Haydn

His Life and Music

www.naxos.com/naxosbooks/haydnlifeandmusic

by David Vickers

Haydn

His Life and Music

Author's Acknowledgements

I am indebted to those who have inspired me to perform, examine and ponder a wide range of eighteenth-century music: Keith Bennett, Robert Blackburn, Julian Rushton, Donald Burrows, Terence Best and the late Stanley Sadie. I thank Genevieve Helsby at Naxos Books for commissioning me to undertake such an enjoyable project. My affection for Haydn's music stems directly from one person: Stephen Fairlie, who was Head of Performance Studies at the music department of Bath College of Higher Education (now Bath Spa University) for only one academic year (1994–5). Stephen gave massive encouragement to me as a fledgling tenor, and encouraged me to learn 'In native worth' from The Creation *during a term in which our choir was preparing to perform the oratorio at the Assembly Rooms in Bath. Tragically, Stephen was killed in a car crash on the way to conduct the last choral rehearsal. The concert was postponed until the beginning of the next academic year, and was an emotional occasion. This book is dedicated to Stephen, with profound thanks for the short but meaningful musical influence he has had on my life. I also 'co-dedicate' this book to my wife Alex, whose encouragement, support and love makes an enormous difference to every project I tackle.*

Published by Naxos Books, an imprint of Naxos Rights International Ltd

© Naxos Books 2008

www.naxosbooks.com

Printed and bound in China by Leo Paper Group

Design and layout: Hannah Davies, Fruition – Creative Concepts

All illustrations © Lebrecht Music & Arts Photo Library (except back
cover image)

Edited by Richard Wigmore

Front cover picture: A portrait of Haydn by Thomas Hardy, 1792

Front cover background picture: View of the palace and gardens at
Eszterháza

Title page picture: A portrait of Haydn by Ludwig Guttenbrunn, c. 1770

A CIP Record for this book is available from the British Library.

ISBN: 978-1-84379-231-4

Contents

www.naxos.com/naxosbooks/haydnlifeandmusic

Visit the dedicated website for *Haydn: His Life and Music* and gain free access to the following:

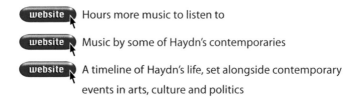

website ▸ Hours more music to listen to

website ▸ Music by some of Haydn's contemporaries

website ▸ A timeline of Haydn's life, set alongside contemporary events in arts, culture and politics

To access this you will need:

- ISBN: 9781843792314
- Password: Farewell

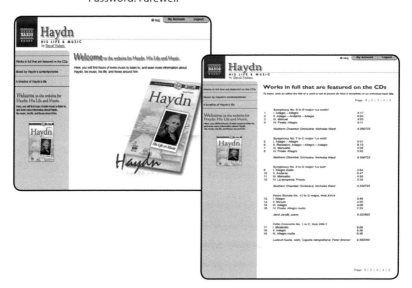

www.naxos.com/naxosbooks/haydnlifeandmusic

Preface

Undertaking a biography of Haydn is impossible without acknowledging the phenomenal scholarship of H.C. Robbins Landon, whose five-volume *Haydn: Chronicle and Works* (published in the 1970s by Thames & Hudson) contains an abundance of fascinating source material and a wealth of insightful guidance on Haydn's life and music. Documentary information about Haydn is rich, but not without its problems: there is very little evidence about him prior to his appointment at the Esterházy court in 1761 other than his autobiographical letter of 1776 and short biographies written by friends soon after his death. A large number of documents in the Esterházy archives relating to the years 1761 to 1779 were destroyed in a fire at Eszterháza in 1779. Many anecdotes and quotations included here derive from Georg August Griesinger, whose biography, based on first-hand conversations with Haydn, was published in Leipzig in 1810.

   This book is divided into chapters dealing with each significant period of Haydn's life and career, which inevitably means that chapters detailing his prolific and enormously successful visits to London, or the years during which he composed *The Creation* and *The Seasons*, are longer than those covering his earlier years. Pertinent summaries of Haydn's achievements in major musical genres are to be found at the end of the main text: symphonies, concertos, keyboard music, string quartets, operas, church music and oratorios. Throughout this biography Hoboken's catalogue numbers are used to identify Haydn's compositions, with the exception of operas and oratorios (whose titles are deemed sufficient) and symphonies (whose established numerical order is taken from Hoboken). German titles of oratorios are given in their English form, but the original-language titles for German and Italian music dramas and Haydn's masses are retained.

Chapter 1

Childhood and Youth, 1732–1749

Childhood and Youth, 1732–1749

After the Turkish retreat from Vienna in September 1683, following their unsuccessful siege, the political landscape of Austria underwent enormous change. Under the Habsburg emperor Charles VI, Austria spread its rule across large parts of Hungary, and with it came reinforcement of the cultural emblems of the Catholic Counter-Reformation: Italianate architecture, art and music were nurtured across the Austro-Hungarian Empire, from the Habsburg court (most of the imperial family were talented musicians) to the country estates of aristocratic families. Life was much more modest for ordinary working people, especially in poverty-stricken rural areas that had been decimated by the Turks. Haydn's grandfather Thomas (c. 1657–1701), a wheelwright, had been one of the lucky few to escape the bloodbath at the hands of the Turkish army that swept through the town of Hainburg (across the Danube from Bratislava) on 12 July 1683. His sixth child, Matthias (1699–1763), also became a skilled wheelwright, and settled at the nearby market village of Rohrau.

Situated twenty-five miles east of Vienna on the west bank of the Leitha river (which marked the border between Austria and Hungary), and eleven miles south of the Danube, Rohrau was the centre of a rural area owned by Count Karl Anton Harrach, whose castle continues to dominate the landscape

today. The area was principally German-speaking, but with *Haydn's birthplace:* an ethnic blend of Croats, Hungarians and Slovaks. Matthias *the house at Rohrau* Haydn was an eminent man in the local community, owing to his role as village magistrate, and in 1728 he married Anna Maria Koller (1707–1754), who had formerly worked as a cook at the castle. The Haydn family lived in a small house, in which Anna Maria gave birth to twelve children, five of whom died in infancy.

Their eldest son was born on 31 March 1732, and baptised at the little parish church the next day. As was often customary in such a strongly Catholic society, the baby boy was given the name of the two saints with proximate feast days: Franz (after Francis of Paola; 2 April) and Joseph (the husband of the Virgin Mary; 19 March). However, the name 'Franz' was seldom ever used. Joseph Haydn, commonly known as 'Sepperl', was exposed to musical activity from an early age. His mother liked singing, and his father was a natural tenor who, despite not being able to read music, enjoyed accompanying himself

3

Michael Haydn

on a harp that he might have acquired when he spent some time working in Frankfurt. This domestic music-making and the organisation of amateur concerts in the village left a firm imprint on the three sons who survived into adulthood. All became professional musicians: Joseph's brother Michael (christened Johann Michael on 14 September 1737) also became a respected composer, and a colleague of the Mozarts at the Salzburg court; the youngest brother Johann Evangelist (1743–1805) became a professional tenor in various choirs.

By the age of five or six Joseph was a talented singer, and legend has it that the young boy pretended to play the violin by scraping a stick against his arm. This attracted the attention of Johann Mathias Franck, a distant cousin and schoolmaster at Hainburg. Franck induced Matthias Haydn to let his young son live with him at Hainburg, where he could receive a better basic education and gain some musical training at the local church where Franck was in charge of music. The Haydn family agreed because they entertained hopes that this might enhance Joseph's chances of taking holy orders. The boy received instruction in literacy, the catechism, singing, almost all kinds of available wind and string instruments, and even the timpani. He is reported to have said in later life: 'I shall owe it to [Franck] to my dying day that he taught me so many things, though in the process I received more thrashings than food.'

Few reliable documents survive about Haydn's early education and musical training, but in an autobiographical letter written in 1776 for an Austrian magazine the forty-four-year-old composer recalled that he was endowed with 'such proficiency that even in my 6th year I was able to sing some Masses in the choir-loft, and to play a little on the harpsichord and violin'. But it seems that the boy's great opportunity to become educated came at a price. He later described his domestic circumstances under Franck's so-called 'care':

> My parents, you see, had accustomed me from my earliest youth to discipline concerning cleanliness and order, and these two things became second nature to me. At Franck's, I couldn't help noticing, very early on, and greatly to my distress, that I was getting dirty, and though I thought rather highly of my little person, I was not always able to avoid getting stains on my clothes, and I was dreadfully ashamed. The fact is, I'm afraid, that I became a regular little ragamuffin.

In about 1740 an event occurred which was to transform Haydn's life. Georg Reutter, Kapellmeister at St Stephen's Cathedral in Vienna since 1738, was travelling around the provinces in search of talented boy singers when a friend in Hainburg told him of an exceptional eight-year-old. Joseph was summoned for an audition, during which he was bribed with a handful of cherries to try singing a trill for the first time. Reutter was impressed with the boy's ability to sing in Latin and Italian, and it was agreed that he become one of six fully funded choral scholars at the prestigious choir school in the Imperial capital. One of the boy's first experiences of singing at St Stephen's Cathedral might have been for the elaborate funeral of Emperor Charles VI, who had died on 20 October 1740 (and was succeeded by his daughter Maria Theresa, thus triggering the eight-year-long War of Austrian Succession). He probably sang in another grand requiem service for the composer Johann Joseph Fux, who was Hofkapellmeister at the Habsburg court until his death, at the age of eighty, on

13 February 1741. Until he was seventeen, Haydn lived with five other boy choristers in the Kapellhaus adjacent to the cathedral. His daily work was dominated by music associated with the liturgical needs of the cathedral. The ordinary daily service typically required a short mass, usually called a *missa brevis*, which was probably performed by a small group handpicked from the available pool of singers and players. The musical establishment at St Stephen's also contained nine other vocalists, three 'Extra-Vocalisten', a 'Subcantor', and instrumentalists that included the organist and composer Anton Reckh, eleven string players, one cornettist and one bassoonist. Trumpets, trombones and kettledrums (timpani) were recruited from the Imperial Trumpeters when necessary for the more opulently scaled *missa solemnis* performed on feast days and special occasions.

Haydn continued to be educated in customary subjects such as Latin, religion, arithmetic and writing, but was now also taught singing by several respected professional teachers, gained mastery of the harpsichord (fortepianos were not yet widely known or used), and became an accomplished violinist. He was thoroughly immersed in performing liturgical chant and music by eminent masters, including Alessandro Scarlatti, Palestrina and Allegri. Most of the repertoire he sang was destroyed when the cathedral was bombed in 1945 during the latter stages of World War II, although music preserved at the Gesellschaft der Musikfreunde reveals that the choirboy Joseph certainly sang plenty of works composed by musicians currently or recently associated with the flourishing musical life at Vienna, including Reutter, Wagenseil, Caldara and Fux. It is unlikely that he knew much about the Baroque masters Bach and Handel – both still very active in the late 1730s and early 1740s – until much later in his life. He may, at nine years old, have been one of the six choral scholars from St Stephen's who sang at Vivaldi's funeral in Vienna's Bürgerspital cemetery on 28 July 1741; but it is nevertheless unlikely that he knew much about the music written by the Venetian 'Red Priest', whose fame and health had both declined as he chased his dwindling operatic fortunes.

Haydn received little formal instruction in musical theory or composition from Reutter, but the eager youth was encouraged to improvise variations according to his own taste when singing solo motets in church services. Participation for almost a decade in performances of high-calibre music by the finest musical institution in Vienna must have had an enormous impact upon the impressionable young musician. He began to imagine himself as a composer, although he later reminisced:

> In those days I used to think everything is fine so long as the paper was well covered. Reutter laughed about my immature products, about movements which no throat and no instrument could have executed, and he scolded me for composing in sixteen parts before I had learnt how to write in two.

Joseph became principal treble soloist at the choir school. In later life he often related that his voice was sufficiently admired for the director of the choir school to propose that he be castrated, in order to give him the chance of an illustrious career as a 'castrato'. His father disapproved, forbade the operation, and hastily visited Vienna to ensure that no harm had come to his son. Haydn had a lucky escape in several ways: not only was castrating boys to preserve their unbroken voices a physically painful and dangerous process, and a barbaric act condemning its victim to live unmarried and childless, but the dominance of castrati in opera faded towards the end of the eighteenth century. Even in its heyday the operation was a gamble, without any guarantee that the adult male would have an adequate voice to make a living as a singer, much less become a famous opera star.

During his teens it was probably part of Joseph's duties to instruct less experienced choirboys in fundamental musical studies, perhaps including his younger brother Michael, who joined the choir school at St Stephen's Cathedral in 1745. Both brothers regularly vexed Kapellmeister Reutter with their mischievous antics. During Pentecost services in 1745 at the royal palace of Schönbrunn, then still under construction, Joseph decided to climb the scaffolding and play noisy, childish games; he was caught by the Empress Maria Theresa, who had him thrashed. Michael, on a visit to Vienna in 1801, is reported to have stopped outside the Kapellhaus (demolished two years later), and nostalgically remarked that he had here received one 'schilling' (i.e. thrashing) every week during his childhood. Playing jokes seems convincingly in character for Haydn, who reveals so much extrovert humour in his music; and being the cause of disturbance is likewise an apt characteristic for a musician who would later be the principal musical proponent of *Sturm und Drang* ('Storm and Stress'). Yet his nineteenth-century biographer Carl Ferdinand Pohl claimed that the composer told a group of choirboys visiting Vienna in 1808 that he had been a diligent student, often taking a portable clavichord up to the attic in order to practise undisturbed while his fellow pupils played outside. One suspects that the elderly 'Papa' Haydn was encouraging the youngsters to be dutiful rather than giving an accurate report of his own childhood.

In his autobiographical letter of 1776 Haydn reminisced that he sang soprano at St Stephen's Cathedral and the imperial court until his '18th year', when his voice began to

break. An anecdote reports that the Empress unkindly (but *St Stephen's* perhaps accurately) observed that 'Joseph Haydn doesn't sing *Cathedral, Vienna* anymore; he crows'. It was inevitable that nature would take its course, and the seventeen-year-old was replaced as the leading treble soloist by Michael, five years his junior. Reutter, allegedly irritated when the teenage Joseph cut off another boy's long hair as a prank, was no longer able to justify the expense of keeping him at the choir school and dismissed his protégé in about November 1749. Although Reutter's decision might seem cruel, Haydn would have expected this to happen eventually. He was not naïve to the fact that puberty had affected other boys at St Stephen's during the last decade. Although reputedly penniless, he was adamant that he would not follow his parents' reiterated desire for him to enter the priesthood. His decision not to return home to Rohrau implies that he was confident of making a life for himself as a professional musician in Vienna.

Chapter 2

Apprenticeship, the Morzins and the Esterházys, 1750–1761

"It was the first time I had ever seen such a sight; I became confused, my playing faltered, my fingers became glued to the keys.
"

Apprenticeship, the Morzins and the Esterházys, 1750–1761

Life was difficult for Haydn after leaving the choir school at St Stephen's Cathedral. He was so plagued by hunger that, against all inclination, he considered taking monastic vows with the Servite Order in order to find food. Fortunately, he benefited from the generosity of several friends. The lacemaker Johann Wilhelm Buchholz lent him 150 gulden – an amount close to a year's salary for an ordinary court musician – without charging interest (Haydn repaid the favour with a bequest in his will to Buchholz's granddaughter). Johann Michael Spangler, a tenor at the Michaelerkirche (near the Imperial palace), offered him accommodation in a garret room at the Michaelerhaus. This was shared with Spangler's wife and infant son, where the cramped conditions (there was no stove, and the roof leaked) must have been far from ideal, especially when Spangler's wife became pregnant with their second child Magdalena (in 1768 Haydn would hire Magdalena Spangler as a soprano at the Esterházy court).

Unlike most prodigious composers during the eighteenth century, Haydn was a late developer as a composer. Few early works have survived, although a *Missa brevis* in F (Hob. XXII:1) for two sopranos and chorus dated 1749 is extant (it might have been intended for Joseph and his brother Michael to sing at the choir school). It was probably in spring 1750 that Haydn visited the enormous Benedictine pilgrimage church at Mariazell in Styria, taking with him several motets that he had written. The fledgling composer hoped the choir would perform his music, although it seems his request was refused.

Haydn had probably begun already to establish a network of useful musical and social contacts in Vienna that helped him to receive an income from playing, singing and teaching. In his autobiographical account of this period written in 1776, he described:

> *When my voice finally broke, for eight whole years I was forced to eke out a wretched existence by teaching young people. Many geniuses are ruined by this miserable [need to earn their] daily bread, because they lack time to study. This could well have happened to me; I would never have achieved what little I have done, had I not carried on with my zeal for composition during the night. I composed diligently, but not quite correctly, until I finally had the good fortune to learn the true fundamentals of composition from the famous Porpora (who was in Vienna at the time).*

Although living conditions in the Michaelerhaus were indeed miserable, Haydn's residency there led to lucky and profitable acquaintances. The imperial court poet Pietro Metastasio lived on the ground floor. Metastasio was famous all over Europe as the leading librettist of the age, whose texts were set by every important operatic composer during the eighteenth century, from Handel to Mozart. Metastasio was acting as a tutor for Marianna von Martines, and the poet arranged for Haydn to give the young lady instruction in playing the harpsichord and singing. In return, the young musician received free board for three years.

Through Metastasio, he met celebrated opera composer Nicola Porpora (1686–1768). Associated with prestigious operatic activity at Naples, Venice, London (in competition with Handel from 1733 to 1736) and Dresden, Porpora was a respected singing teacher who had taught the famous castrato Farinelli. From late 1752 or early 1753, Porpora was based in Vienna and greatly in demand as a singing teacher for the aristocracy. Porpora paid Haydn to accompany his singing pupils at the keyboard, and the aspiring composer even worked as Porpora's valet during a summer trip to the popular spa resort of Bad Mannersdorf. Haydn remembered Porpora as a difficult taskmaster:

> There was no lack of Ass, Blockhead, Rascal and pokes in the ribs, but I willingly put up with it all, for I profited immensely from Porpora in singing, composition and Italian.

Porpora and Metastasio introduced Haydn to important composers, including Gluck and Wagenseil (Wagenseil's approval of his musicianship was particularly encouraging). It is also likely that Haydn was introduced to Metastasio's close friend Hasse during one of the composer's visits to Vienna. All such contacts with influential elders were essential for an aspiring young composer. He eagerly absorbed scholarly treatises about music, too, including Mattheson's *Der vollkommene Capellmeister* (1739). He particularly studied Fux's famous theoretical work *Gradus ad Parnassum* (1725), annotated his copy in Latin, made Fux's ideas the basis of his own later teaching of composition, and continued to refer to it with admiration throughout the rest of his long life.

During the mid-1750s things improved for Haydn. He continued to be active as a church musician. Some Sundays were phenomenally busy: he led the orchestra at the convent chapel of the Barmherzige Brüder (a holy order) at eight o'clock in the morning (for which he was paid sixty gulden a year), played the organ at the private chapel of Count Haugwitz in the Bohemian Court Chancellery on the Wipplingerstrasse at ten o'clock, and an hour later was singing with his old choir at St Stephen's Cathedral (where he was paid one gulden for each service). Records show that Haydn was paid to be an extra singer at the Hofkapelle during Lent in 1754, 1755 and 1756. He was also employed by the court as a casual violinist, playing at special balls arranged for the children of the imperial family and their friends during carnival season in 1755 and 1756, for which he was paid four gulden an evening.

Haydn and fellow musicians gained a reputation for continuing the sort of mischievous antics that had got Haydn into trouble as a schoolboy. The musicians often played in outdoor serenades ('Nachtmusik'), but Haydn's friend and biographer Albert Christoph Dies relates that for one occasion Haydn decided to secretly invite a number of musicians to meet in the Tiefer Graben, give them different positions on the street – including a kettledrummer on the bridge – and tell each of them to play whatever they wanted. The ensuing cacophony was not appreciated by local residents, who threw open their windows and shouted, hissed and whistled at the confused musicians. Two of the players were arrested by the watchmen, but both were set free when neither could explain who the ringleader was.

However, most evening serenades were more refined affairs, and it was for one such occasion in 1753 that Haydn probably composed his Cassation in G for string quintet (Hob.II:2). He also participated in chamber-music parties in his home town of Rohrau, which granted him opportunities to visit his family (although his mother died on

21 February 1754, and his father remarried on 19 July 1755). An eyewitness reported that on these occasions Haydn 'was modest to the point of timidity, despite the fact that everybody present was enchanted'.

Although it is difficult to establish the exact chronology of Haydn's works written during the 1750s, he swiftly became an indefatigable composer working in many different genres. Haydn was not yet involved with any Italian opera projects, notwithstanding his experience of it obtained from Metastasio and Porpora, but during the 1750s the taste of the imperial court moved towards French-style opera, with which Haydn seems to have felt little affinity. It was through performing an outdoor serenade that he met Joseph Felix von Kurz, a comic actor (whose stage name was 'Bernardon') responsible for a troupe of actors and singers who performed German opera at the Kärtnertortheater. It was for this group that Haydn composed his first music for the stage, *Der krumme Teufel* ('The Crooked Devil', c. 1751–2) and *Der neue krumme Teufel* (c. 1759), although no music survives from either opera. In addition to serenade music for mixed ensembles, he was requested to write music for string quartets and divertimentos. Most of his keyboard sonatas and trios written during this period were intended as teaching materials, taking into consideration the abilities of his pupils. He initially charged pupils two gulden a month for lessons, but gradually his reputation increased enough for him to raise his fees to five gulden a month. He attracted some affluent keyboard and singing pupils, such as the elder Countess Maria Christine Thun, and taught aspiring professional musicians such as Robert Kimmerling, later the director of music at the Benedictine Abbey in Melk.

Haydn also gave music lessons to the daughters of the wigmaker Johann Peter Keller, whose younger brother Georg

Ignaz Keller was a violinist at St Stephen's Cathedral. He fell deeply in love with the youngest daughter Therese. Her parents welcomed him openly into their home for meals and allegedly desired nothing better than for him to become their son-in-law; but nothing could dissuade them from their resolution that Therese should become a nun at the Convent of the Poor Clares. In accordance with her parents' wishes, she entered the nunnery in 1755, and on 12 May 1756 took her formal solemn vows. The music for the ceremony was dutifully provided and directed by Haydn: it is very likely that two splendid works, an Organ Concerto in C (Hob.XVIII:1) and a *Salve regina* in E (Hob.XXIIIb:1), were both created especially for this occasion. Although there is no hint of the twenty-four-year-old composer's heartbreak in his radiantly affirmative music, he carefully kept the autographs of both works for the rest of his life, later dating them both 1756, as if to underscore their sentimental value to him.

Haydn moved to new accommodation in the Seilerstätte, but must have suffered anxiety about his future when his possessions were stolen. Griesinger described how the composer's father came to Vienna to give his son a seventeen-kreuzer coin, and the advice 'Fear God, and love thy neighbour!' Again, good friends were able to help the composer to recover: one gave him shirts and underclothing, another had a suit made for him, and he was invited to stay as a guest for two months with his near neighbour and patron, Baron Carl Joseph Fürnberg. Haydn taught music to Fürnberg's children in Vienna, but the Baron also had a country estate at Weinzierl where he liked to make music informally with his estate manager, a local musician and the parish priest. It was for this group that Fürnberg commissioned Haydn to compose his first string quartets (perhaps including Op. 1 No. 1) sometime between 1755 and

Schloss Weinzierl,
home to the
Fürnberg family

1757. They were so pleased with Haydn's initial experiments that he was encouraged to continue cultivating his efforts in the genre.

In 1757 or 1758 Fürnberg recommended Haydn for the post of music director for a member of the aristocratic Morzin family, who lived in the Batthyany palace in Vienna. The composer was paid an annual salary of 200 gulden, granted free lodging, and was permitted to take meals at the officers' table. Now in his mid-twenties, at last he was appointed to an official position that allowed him free rein to write music as part of his expected duties; Griesinger claims that Haydn was finally able to enjoy a carefree existence. He would have been expected to accompany the family during summers at their palace at Lukavec in Bohemia, and perhaps on occasional visits to their small palace in Prague. In later years, Haydn would be fond of relating how he was one day sitting at the harpsichord and the beautiful Countess Morzin leant over him in order to see the notes better. Her neckerchief came undone, and her inadvertent display of cleavage apparently caused the young Haydn to become distracted from his duties:

It was the first time I had ever seen such a sight; I became confused, my playing faltered, my fingers became glued to the keys. 'What is that, Haydn, what are you doing?' cried the Countess; most respectfully I answered: 'But, Countess, your grace, who would not be undone at such a sight?'

The only other incident from this period that the elderly Haydn described to his biographers was falling off a horse, but it was certainly at around this time that he composed his first symphony (perhaps No. 1 in D major). He had an orchestra at his personal disposal for the first time, although it is not clear whether he directed it from the violin or from the harpsichord. He composed at least fourteen more symphonies for the Morzins, and also concertos, divertimentos (including Hob.XIV:11), partitas for windband, string trios, probably some of the Op. 2 string quartets, and keyboard sonatas (including Hob.XVI:6). Though officially titled Morzin's Kapellmeister, it seems Haydn's duties excluded the provision of music for chapel services. His compositional activity was devoted to domestic entertainment for his patrons, and presumably musical performances at special social occasions. Some of the music that the Morzin orchestra performed included commissions from Haydn's younger brother Michael, who after leaving the choir school received an excellent education from the Jesuits, and also became a talented composer in his own right (he would eventually obtain an appointment at the court of the Prince-Archbishop of Salzburg, where he would remain for most of his life).

Joseph was probably permitted to continue his freelance activities when the Morzin family spent the winter months in Vienna. He maintained his friendship with the Keller family, and five years after Therese had entered the nunnery, he married her elder sister Maria Anna at St Stephen's Cathedral on 26 November 1760. We can only speculate as to why Haydn made this decision. It is possible that his sense of duty and gratitude towards the Kellers played a large part, but it might have been that Maria Anna was the closest equivalent to Therese (now renamed Sister Josepha) that he could find. We cannot rule out the possibility that he was attracted to Maria Anna in her own right, but Griesinger remarks that she 'kept pressing the matter' of marriage until Haydn relented. The biographer also describes her as 'a domineering, unfriendly character', a bigot and spendthrift. It was an unhappy marriage. It is alleged that Maria Anna used Haydn's music manuscripts as curling papers for her hair, and as underlays for her pastries. He later blamed their troubled relationship and mutual infidelity on the fact they could not have children, but that surely is a partial and self-interested explanation. Their marriage certificate refers to Haydn as 'Music Director with Count v. Morzin', but Morzin's enthusiasm had led him to spend more on maintaining his musical establishment than he could afford. Shortly after the wedding, probably in spring 1761, the Count was obliged to dissolve his orchestra and release Haydn from his employment.

The potentially disastrous consequences for the newlyweds were averted because Haydn's work at Count Morzin's had attracted the keen attention of an eminent guest: Prince Paul Anton Esterházy was a passionate patron of the arts, a capable musician, and the head of an influential Hungarian family. The Esterházys' ancestry has been traced back to the Hungarian occupation of Bratislava in the late ninth century, and during the early 1600s the head of the family was elected Palatine by his fellow Hungarian nobles. Through political alliances and shrewd marriages the family became wealthy: its accumulated estates were larger than many German principalities during the eighteenth century, and each generation was intensively involved in cultural patronage. The family was loyal to the Austrian Habsburgs, especially during a Hungarian rebellion against the imperial rulers in 1670; and in 1687 Count Paul Esterházy was rewarded by Emperor Leopold I with the title of Prince of the Holy Roman Empire. Shortly before Paul's death the rank of prince was made hereditary by Charles IV, and thereafter the eldest son of the family inherited the title automatically. Paul Anton Esterházy inherited it in June 1721, when he was only ten years old. The fourth prince of the dynasty, Paul Anton came of age in 1734, and promptly served in the Habsburg army. A staunch defender of Empress Maria Theresa in the War of Austrian Succession (1740–8), Paul Anton was appointed her ambassador to Naples for several years, and later rose to the rank of Field Marshal during the Seven Years War (1756–63). Paul Anton was well educated at Vienna and Leyden, and became an intellectual who possessed a consuming interest in literature and music (he played the flute, violin and lute). Since 1728 the Esterházy musical establishment had been efficiently managed by Gregor Joseph Werner, but by early 1761 the infirm Kapellmeister was no longer capable of fulfilling his duties. Paul Anton wished to modernise and enlarge the court music, and, upon hearing one of Haydn's symphonies at Count Morzin's, recognised the twenty-eight-year-old musician as an ideally brilliant candidate to assist (and eventually replace) Werner.

Haydn was employed at Prince Paul Anton's Viennese residence on the Wallnerstrasse from mid-March 1761. He was informally appointed vice-Kapellmeister by 1 April, and this prestigious appointment was formalised with a three-year extendable contract signed on 1 May. This contract was necessarily diplomatic towards the conservative Werner, kindly acknowledging that he had devoted many years of diligent service, and specifying:

> *Gregorius Werner, in consideration of his long service, shall continue to serve, as Ober-Kapellmeister... Joseph Haydn, as vice-Kapellmeister, shall be subordinate... in regard to the choral music in Eisenstadt; but in all other circumstances where any sort of music is to be made, everything pertaining to the music, in general and in particular, is the responsibility of said vice-Kapellmeister.*

Haydn was fully aware that many able musicians died in abject poverty, and therefore would have been reassured and impressed to witness how his new patron respected the elderly Werner, who had worked for the Esterházys for nearly thirty-three years. Werner remained in charge of providing new church music at the family's principal summer home in Eisenstadt (a small town twenty-six miles south-east of Vienna), but his new vice-Kapellmeister was responsible for everything else, including assisting Paul Anton to reorganise his group of 'princely musicians'. Haydn probably chose instrumentalists whom he knew from Vienna, perhaps including some who had been part of his old orchestra disbanded by Count Morzin. His extensive duties included composing all secular vocal, stage and instrumental music according to the Prince's demands, as well as teaching singing, hiring and managing the court's musicians (both professionally and domestically), keeping the archive of musical performance material in good order, and the purchase and upkeep of instruments (players in the Esterházy orchestra did not own their own instruments). He was contractually obliged to perform both as leader and as soloist whenever required, and instructed to appear before the Prince twice daily (morning and afternoon) to receive instructions about whether music was desired. Any external work he undertook as a performer or composer had to be agreed with the 'gracious consent' of the Prince. The contract concluded with the promise that should Haydn 'provide complete satisfaction, he may look forward to the position of Oberkapellmeister'.

At last granted a secure position, the vice-Kapellmeister earned 400 gulden a year, and enjoyed a status as a 'house officer' (a rank above that of servant) which entitled him to free lodgings, meals at the officers' table, and an elaborate uniform of blue with gold trimmings. Griesinger informs us that Haydn's aged father was delighted to witness his son wearing the uniform, and to hear the Prince enthusing about his son's talents. Notwithstanding the enormous amount of hard work and responsibility that his position entailed, Haydn flourished in an environment in which he could adventurously experiment with performers of remarkably high proficiency, and gain intense experience of creating and performing music in many genres. Prince Paul Anton was an enthusiast for Italianate music and is known to have possessed scores of Vivaldi's music, including *The Four Seasons*. Familiarity with such music might have influenced the Prince to make interesting suggestions for musical projects. Dies writes that Paul Anton 'gave Haydn the four periods of the day [morning, noon, evening, night] as the theme of a composition'. The resulting symphonies – 'Le Matin' (Symphony No. 6), 'Le Midi' (Symphony No. 7) and 'Le Soir' (Symphony No. 8) – were probably Haydn's first original compositions for the Esterházy family, in whose service he would remain for the rest of his life.

23

Influences and Early Style

No successful eighteenth-century composer wrote music out of purely isolated artistic motivation; the main purpose of composition was to earn an income. However, Haydn notably sought to use subtle expression, graceful melodies and original harmonic ideas to charm, delight and, most importantly, move the sentiments of the listener. This reinforces his artistic and historical alignment with Mozart, but it is too easy for us to forget that Haydn belonged to the previous generation of composers. The 'Classical' (or 'galant') style was developed by many mid-eighteenth-century composers whose legacy came directly from what we now describe as 'High Baroque'. It is highly unlikely that the young Haydn knew music by J.S. Bach or Handel, but Vivaldi's orchestral music was reasonably popular, and he certainly sang, played and knew music and writings by composers who descended from the same technical background (Alessandro Scarlatti, Fux, Mattheson, Caldara, Wagenseil, and C.P.E. Bach).

Although style changed rapidly across Europe during the mid-eighteenth century, the old techniques, structures, devices and ideology that had been understood and developed in the early eighteenth century remained fundamental to Haydn's self-taught education as a composer in the late 1750s. It was considered necessary to first have a sound understanding and mastery of the rules of musical invention before being able to play with them and perhaps even stretch them further. A good composer was expected to have a thorough grasp of strict counterpoint and harmony, be able to master the pivotal role of improvised keyboard continuo in vocal music (organ in church, and harpsichord in the theatre or ballroom), know the unwritten musical language of embellishment in both instrumental and vocal performance (such as appoggiaturas, trills, ornamentation of repeated material, and improvised cadenzas towards the final section of a piece), and have a full command of the theoretical ideas about what formed good taste and judgement. Likewise, aesthetics common in Baroque music – such as theatrical rhetoric in declamatory phrasing of opening statements, finely spun polyphony, virtuosity of solo parts (both vocal or instrumental) and intricacy – remained essential in the Classical style.

James Webster summed up Haydn's musical style as based on a 'principle of variety within unity... both novelty and continuity are maintained from beginning to end'. This is evident from his earliest extant compositions in all genres, although they might be described with hindsight as 'progressive Baroque' music, in which the musical vocabulary we associate with the mature Haydn and Mozart (and early Beethoven) has not yet developed. Although undeniably an innovator, and often justifiably referred to as the father of the symphony and the string quartet, Haydn was not the first composer to write music in those genres, nor did he develop his style in a vacuum. Close contemporaries such as Boccherini, Sammartini, Gassmann, Dittersdorf and Vanhal were also stylistic pioneers, and he would certainly have benefited from their musical explorations, just as many of them would also benefit from his own.

In the late 1750s and early 1760s the fortepiano, then in its infancy, had not yet superseded the harpsichord, and orchestras tended to be small and simply constituted, often with just two oboes, two horns and four-part strings (with double bass doubling the cello part). In Haydn's early compositions (such as symphonies Nos 6–8), his music reveals an imaginative use of reduced textures, adventurous solo lines, brilliant upper-register writing (e.g. solo soprano voices in church music; violins in symphonies), strongly characterised bass lines, astute use of colour and timing for dramatic effect (e.g. punctuating horns), and clever use of sonata form. Two fast movements usually flank a central slower movement, although frequently Haydn is flexible with form, and sometimes uses an alternating scheme of slow–fast–slow–fast movements (known as *da chiesa*, after church sonatas by old Italian composers such as Corelli).

Chapter 3

'I had to become original': Eisenstadt and Eszterháza, 1762–1775

'I had to become original': Eisenstadt and Eszterháza, 1762–1775

Haydn's relationship with his supportive new employer was short. Prince Paul Anton Esterházy's rapidly deteriorating health influenced his decision to remain in Vienna during summer 1761 instead of making the customary tour around his several country palaces. Although happily married for many years, the Prince and his wife did not have children, and upon Paul Anton's death on 18 March 1762 he was succeeded by his brother Nicolaus. This was by no means bad for Haydn: Prince Nicolaus I (known in his own day as 'Nicolaus the Magnificent') had received the same excellent education as his late brother, and achieved comparable respect as a Lieutenant Field Marshall in the Habsburg army. The second and most lavish of the four Esterházy princes whom Haydn served, Nicolaus was widely known across the Holy Roman Empire for his ostentatious splendour and fondness for culture, which led him to nurture painting, sculpture, architecture and music to an extent that outshone the imperial family.

Prince Nicolaus Esterházy I

Prince Nicolaus was also a shrewd and scrupulously fair manager of his family's many estates, which included palaces at Pressburg (now Bratislava) and Kittsee. The court would move to various locations from time to time, but from 1762 to 1765 Nicolaus lived primarily at the family's main home at the castle in Eisenstadt (the family did not own the surrounding town, although they had enormous influence over it and frequently contributed to the development of important buildings). Originally built in the thirteenth century, the castle was bought by an ancestor of Prince Nicolaus in 1647. Between 1663 and 1672 the castle was rebuilt by Italian architects as a Baroque palace, which included a grand hall where a century later Haydn directed the court orchestra in performances of his new works. Now renamed the Haydnsaal, the hall has a resonant acoustic almost like that of a church; as some scholars have noted, it may have influenced Haydn's instrumentation in his symphonies and concertos. Spoken drama and operas were performed in a theatre constructed in a glass house in the gardens, which Prince Paul Anton had built in 1761 with advice from the impresario Count Giacomo Durazzo (who was soon to commission Gluck and the librettist Calzabigi to create the *festa teatrale Orfeo ed Euridice* for Vienna's Burgtheater).

Haydn's orchestra (known as the 'Capelle') gradually grew from an initially modest size. At first it consisted of no more than fifteen players, many of whom were skilled at more than one instrument. There were about six violinists, individual viola, cello and double bass players, a flautist, two oboists, a pair of horn players, and a bassoonist (who often played the cello and double bass part). Throughout the 1760s and 1770s the Capelle expanded, and at its peak in the 1780s it featured at least twenty-two musicians. Although Haydn played keyboard continuo in opera performances, he normally directed instrumental concerts from the violin. However, the prominent virtuoso violin solos in many of his orchestral

The Bergkirche at Eisenstadt, where Haydn was eventually buried

works were played by the concertmaster Luigi Tomasini. This Italian violinist had worked as a valet for the Esterházys since the early 1750s and was officially put on the payroll of musicians at around the same time as Haydn was appointed vice-Kapellmeister; the two musicians became lifelong close friends. All the musicians (including Haydn and his wife) lived in the so-called 'Old Apothecary' next to the Bergkirche, a church that stands just up the hill from the castle.

At first Haydn's duties remained essentially unchanged at Eisenstadt, although Oberkapellmeister Werner seems to have become increasingly jealous of what he perceived as the favouritism the Prince showed towards his protégé. The younger composer appears to have respected Werner, and would later even safeguard a collection of his elder colleague's autograph scores, but perhaps Werner's bitterness was aggravated by Prince Nicolaus raising Haydn's salary to 600 gulden (a fifty percent increase) on 25 June 1762, only a few months after inheriting his title. However, the Prince was delighted with Haydn's fruitful development of high-quality musical performances in Eisenstadt. The composer later reminisced to Griesinger:

> *My prince was pleased with all my work, I received success, I could as head of an orchestra make experiments and observe what made an impression, what weakened it and, in a way, improve, add, delete and experiment. I was cut off from the rest of the world, there was no one in the vicinity to annoy or disturb me, and so I had to become original.*

Haydn's self-professed originality was most evident in about twenty-five symphonies composed during the early 1760s, including the nicknamed works 'The Philosopher' (Symphony No. 22 in E flat, which unusually features two cors anglais instead of oboes), 'Alleluja' (Symphony No. 30 in C major, which quotes a Gregorian Easter chant in its first movement), and the 'Hornsignal' (Symphony No. 31 in D major, in which the Capelle horns were doubled from two to four, and must have brayed in splendid fashion). Most of his output during the early 1760s was instrumental music, although chamber music and keyboard works seem to have played a small part in his duties at Eisenstadt. However, works such as the Keyboard Sonata No. 13 in G major (Hob.XVI:6) probably date from around this time.

Although many works written during this period are now lost, we know that Haydn composed several concertos for Luigi Tomasini. One of these was the Violin Concerto No. 1 in C major, Hob.VIIa:1, which displayed the violinist's brilliance at rapid passagework and his lovely tone in the slower music. The composer also gave the limelight to other members of the Esterházy orchestra in the Cello Concerto in C (Hob.VIIb:1), a horn concerto and several lost works, including a concerto for two horns.

The only notable church music written at around this time was the first of his two *Te Deum* settings (Hob.XXIIIc:1, for an unknown occasion). However, almost a decade after learning about Italianate vocal music first-hand from Porpora, Haydn now had opportunities to compose Italian operas: four comic operas (now lost, apart from fragments of *La marchesa Nespola*, 1762–3) were written for the glass theatre in the castle garden, and in January 1763 the *festa teatrale Acide* was performed to celebrate the marriage of the Prince's eldest son Anton (a lost cantata was also heard at the wedding). Secular works requiring virtuoso singers and instrumentalists were created for special occasions, such as six honorific cantatas (of which three survive) written for Prince Nicolaus's nameday (6 December), his recovery from illness, or his return from distant travels.

In late summer 1763 Matthias Haydn died. With Michael recently established at Salzburg, and Joseph secure in the service of the Esterházys, Matthias's youngest son Johann and his stepmother were the joint-largest beneficiaries of the will. Less financially secure than his more illustrious older brothers, Johann was a tenor chorister who was soon engaged as a singer at the Esterházy court (initially unpaid). A year later, Haydn and the entire Capelle were taken to the Esterházy castle at Kittsee, which required an organ builder from Pressburg (now Bratislava) to overhaul the decrepit harpsichord. Payments and bills from this period show that he was actively engaged in the bureaucratic procedures of managing the Capelle, but by the end of 1764 he had fallen ill. We do not know much about this sickness, but it was serious enough for him to petition Prince Nicolaus to purchase 'necessary medicines'. Despite the Prince's expressed reluctance to set a precedent for other musicians to follow, he authorised this expense on 27 December 1764. Haydn was still not better by 23 January 1765 when he wrote from Eisenstadt to Prince Nicolaus in Vienna, informing him that a new horn player was required to replace a recently deceased member of the Capelle, and adding that 'I have felt bad several times in the past few days, and much worse than before'. He again petitioned the Prince for some money to buy medicines, and it seems that he was fully recovered by spring 1765.

The next year or so was a testing time for the composer. The management and cultivation of his orchestra had hitherto seemed peaceful, but its smooth running was disrupted during late summer 1765 by a tense conflict with the Regent of the Prince's estates, Peter Ludwig von Rahier. The flautist Franz Sigl had accidentally set fire to one of the Prince's houses when trying to shoot at some birds on the roof, and the potentially disastrous spread of the fire across Eisenstadt had only been narrowly prevented. Sigl was arrested and roughly imprisoned by Rahier. Haydn leapt to the defence of Sigl and other musicians who became embroiled in the affair, and attempted to reason with Rahier. Haydn's entreaties were not received well by the stubborn official, a former military man who took any form of complaint from the musicians as insubordination. Rahier spoke offensively to them and slammed the door in Haydn's face. The appalled vice-Kapellmeister felt strong loyalty to his colleagues, and on 9 September 1765 he wrote a polite yet transparently aggrieved letter to Prince Nicolaus about the crisis. He pointed out that it was not Sigl's detention with which he had disagreed, but rather Rahier's unreasonably harsh treatment of Sigl; and he complained about the Regent's rude behaviour towards him and other members of the Capelle. One may imagine that Nicolaus had sympathy for both parties: Haydn's intervention seems to have persuaded the Prince to placate Rahier, and the volatile situation was pacified; but neither could the Prince tolerate foolishness that had jeopardised the entire town, and he dismissed Sigl from his service (some leniency may be inferred from the flautist's re-engagement three years later).

A month after his letter to Prince Nicolaus, Haydn had to answer charges of laxity from the embittered Kapellmeister Werner. The infirm seventy-two-year-old was no longer capable of supervising church music, but had received reports of disorder in the chapel choir. On 8 October 1765 Werner wrote a letter to the Prince, in which he protested that he was forced to draw attention to the gross negligence of Haydn's management, criticised what he felt were unnecessarily large expenses, and attacked the 'lazy idleness' of the whole band, 'for which the principal responsibility must be laid at the door of the present director, who lets them all get away with everything'. He also complained that 'there are only libertines among the chorus people' and that many musicians were frequently absent from the court for unacceptably long periods of time; observed that half of the choir's instruments, bought only seven years ago by Prince Paul Anton, were lost (presumably stolen by their users); and that the music library carefully maintained by the late organist Johann Novotni had been carelessly depleted by unsupervised borrowing for unauthorised use outside the court.

Werner, by now weak and bed-ridden, might have harboured some resentment towards his talented younger deputy, and perhaps he was too eager to believe all the slanderous reports. But while none of the musical instruments was actually missing, Werner's insinuation that the easy-going Haydn was not sufficiently inclined to discipline wayward musicians was probably true. He did not cast aspersion on his younger colleague's musical abilities, and he may have had genuine concern that Haydn needed to sort things out. He made shrewd recommendations to the Prince about how to achieve this:

Your Princely Highness should give him [Haydn] a severe order that he must issue the strictest command to the princely musicians that they appear in the future, all of them without exception, at their duties... Under the late lamented Prince, apart from the usual summer fatigue, it was ordered that in winter time we were to give two academies [concerts] a week in

the princely officers' room, Tuesdays and Thursdays, for which
two hours each was required. If this were to be reinstated now,
the injurious laziness would be removed, and no longer would
such practices obtain as, alas, experience has shown to have
occurred.

Prince Nicolaus was preoccupied with supervising the construction of a spectacular new summer palace on the site of the family's hunting lodge at Süttör, but noted Werner's complaints and instructed Rahier to act on the matter. In late November or early December 1765, Rahier – with some input from the Prince – issued Haydn with a stern reprimand, and instructed him to resolve Werner's complaints using a seven-point directive regarding the conduct and administration of the Capelle. Rahier and Prince Nicolaus ordered that three identical copies be made of a new inventory of the music archives and musical instruments, entitled *Regulatio Chori Kissmartoniensis*, within eight days. The archivist and castle schoolmaster Joseph Dietzl was made responsible for distributing and collecting the necessary music before each chapel service, and also for the supervision and maintenance of the choir instruments. Following Werner's advice, all members of the chapel were ordered to appear regularly at church services and to 'fulfil their duty and obligations in a proper and disciplined fashion'; the twice-weekly 'academies' were reinstated; and it was made clear that any musician's absence without permission from church services or concerts would no longer be tolerated. But it is notable that Prince Nicolaus did not imply any dissatisfaction with Haydn, and seemed less bothered about Werner's complaints than about ensuring his vice-Kapellmeister composed more prolifically. In an eccentric postscript, Haydn was entreated to compose 'more zealously than heretofore', and especially to write more

Haydn's baryton

pieces that could be played on the baryton (an obscure and soon-to-be-obsolete member of the viol family that the Prince had become insatiably fond of since recently acquiring one during a visit to Innsbruck).

Haydn was probably dismayed and angry at Werner's complaints but he responded by attentively following the newly issued directive. Additionally he began to keep a thematic catalogue of his own works (the 'Entwurf-Katalog'), perhaps to demonstrate his orderliness and diligence in composing new music for the court (he would regularly update this catalogue until about 1777, and sporadically thereafter). In particular, he responded to his patron's desire for baryton music. On 4 January 1766 he sent three new trios (for baryton, viola and basso) to the Prince at Süttör, who had only the day before instructed that his new palace should be known as 'Eszterháza'. The delighted Prince awarded the composer twelve gold ducats, and immediately ordered six more trios.

On 3 March 1766 Gregor Werner died, and Haydn was promptly promoted to Kapellmeister. For the last year or so he had already been doing all the work that this senior position entailed and his salary did not change, but now he was officially responsible for church music. Expected to compose large-scale vocal music as part of his formal duties, he was able to show his ability at church music for the first time in a decade. His first solemn mass for the Esterházys was the *Missa Cellensis in honorem BVM* (Hob.XXII:5), which might have been drafted for a Viennese service associated with Mariazell, a pilgrimage church where the family had a side-chapel.

Eszterháza

The change in Haydn's status might have played a part in his decision to purchase a little house in the Klostergasse in Eisenstadt on 2 May 1766 (it is now a museum devoted to the composer). The property was legally attached to several small parcels of land, including a kitchen garden and a modest summer house in which it is said that Haydn sometimes composed. Meanwhile, Prince Nicolaus was growing increasingly fond of spending time at his elaborate architectural work-in-progress, Eszterháza. His decision to have a portion of his entire court (including Haydn and some of the Capelle) stay there during summer 1766 was an indication of things to come. The remote estate, located fifty-three miles south-east of Vienna, and just east of Lake Neusiedl, was in the middle of a reclaimed swamp. The Prince had instigated an ambitious irrigation programme, and from the mid-1760s until 1784 he devoted an enormous amount of energy and money (13,000,000 gulden) to creating a splendid three-storey palace containing 126 rooms (including a chapel), an art gallery, two purpose-built opera houses, a coffee house (containing a billiard table), impressive panoramic formal gardens and extensive parkland with statues, fountains and temples. Only the palace survives today.

Frequently known as the closest Austro-Hungarian equivalent to Versailles (which Prince Nicolaus visited in 1767), Eszterháza was described as follows by a visitor in 1784:

> With the exception of Versailles, there is perhaps no place to compare with it for magnificence. The castle is very large and filled to bursting point with luxurious things. The garden contains everything that human fantasy can conceive to

37

*improve or, if you will, undo the work of nature. Pavilions of
all kinds stand like the dwellings of voluptuous fairies, and
everything is so far removed from the usual human operations
that one looks at it as if in the middle of a marvellous dream.*

The two opera houses at Eszterháza were to play a large part
in Haydn's life over the next two decades: the larger building
(built in 1768) had an audience capacity of 400 and all the
necessary mechanisms for moving scenery and for special
effects such as flying chariots; the smaller 'marionette' puppet
theatre (1773) was built in the style of a grotto, but was large
enough for 'real' opera performances between November
1779 and February 1781, when the larger theatre had to be
rebuilt after its destruction by fire. Haydn's regular activities
as an opera composer started on a modest scale: the witty
single-act opera *La canterina* was probably performed in a
makeshift theatre at Eisenstadt during a visit by the imperial
family, and its first public performance was during a carnival
at Pressburg on 16 February 1767. The new opera house at
Eszterháza was inaugurated during late September 1768
with a performance of Haydn's *Lo speziale*, which set an
adaptation of a libretto by the famous Venetian playwright
Carlo Goldoni. Another Goldoni libretto was used for *Le
pescatrici*, premiered on 16 September 1770 as part of the
celebrations surrounding the wedding of the Prince's niece
Countess Lamberg.

Despite its stunning gardens, opera houses, and several
opulent rooms specially designed for the Prince's concerts,
Eszterháza was not universally loved: the court employees,
including the musicians, disliked its isolation (especially since
their families usually remained behind in Eisenstadt), and the
environment outside the estate was far from congenial. The
visitor quoted above also observed:

Eszterháza

What increases the magnificence of the place is the contrast with the surrounding countryside. Anything more dull or depressing can hardly be imagined... The inhabitants of this country look for the most part like ghosts, and in spring they always get cold fever... Unhealthy as is the country, especially in spring and autumn, and although the Prince himself is attacked by cold fever, he is firmly persuaded that in the whole wide world there is no more healthy and pleasant place.

Prince Nicolaus, who disliked living in towns and only visited Vienna at Christmas to pay his annual respects to the imperial family, increasingly preferred Eszterháza to Eisenstadt. In the meantime his court led a strange double life at both castles. New music continued to be eagerly appreciated by the Prince and generously rewarded with impromptu extra payments. Haydn was producing large-scale church music such as his fine setting of *Stabat mater* (Hob.XXbis, presumably written for Eisenstadt in about 1767, perhaps for Good Friday) as well as small chamber

39

works for the Prince's domestic music-making at Eszterháza (such as more baryton trios), and he continued to write symphonies. The rate at which the Kapellmeister produced instrumental music for the full Capelle slowed down during the late 1760s, but the works themselves increased in quality, duration, and theatrical adventurousness. Many of the most popular symphonies belonging to this period were nicknamed, such as 'Fire' (No. 59 in A major, probably written in 1767, with a notably volatile opening *Presto*), 'Lamentatione' (No. 26 in D minor, c. 1768, which has plainchant integrated into the first two movements and was probably intended for Passiontide), 'La passione' (Symphony No. 49 in F minor, perhaps composed for Holy Week in 1768, and Haydn's last symphony to take the form of an Italianate *sonata da chiesa*), and 'Maria Theresia' (No. 48 in C major, an exuberant ceremonial work written c. 1768–9, in which horns act the part of fanfaring trumpets).

Further to his duties at the court, Haydn was also granted permission to compose large-scale vocal works for other institutions: in about March 1768 he composed the *Applausus* cantata (Hob.XXIVa:6), a congratulatory one-act work in Latin, for the Cistercian Monastery at Zwettl in Lower Austria. He was not able to direct its performance at the monastery, so instead he sent a detailed letter of instructions with the score, requesting that tempo and dynamic markings be strictly observed, and asking that the musicians 'be as diligent as possible'. A few months later Haydn was negotiating the hire of several trumpeters and a timpanist from Oedenburg for an unspecified musical performance on 26 July 1768. Perhaps this was the occasion for which he composed his magnificent new *Missa in honorem BVM* (the 'Grosse Orgelsolomesse', Hob.XXII:4, with a solo organ part played by the composer).

A few weeks later disaster struck once again. On 2 August a fire laid waste to most of the lower part of Eisenstadt. Only nineteen houses in that part of the town survived unscathed, but the Haydns' home on the Klostergasse was devastated by the flames. Haydn had borrowed money to purchase his house, and the serious damage to the building and the loss of its contents (including many unique scores) meant that he and his wife Maria Anna were potentially ruined. Upon hearing of the incident, Prince Nicolaus paid for their house to be rebuilt at his own expense (although the Haydns took the opportunity to add an extra room, for which they had to pay fifty gulden, and there was a subsquent dispute over boundaries with the widow who lived next door). When another tragic destruction by fire occurred in 1776, the Prince responded with exactly the same charity. It was such magnanimous acts that bound Kapellmeister Haydn to his Prince. The composer's music gradually became popular and admired all over Europe, and, although his isolation perhaps made him unaware of his fame, it is easy to perceive why he remained steadfastly loyal to Prince Nicolaus Esterházy.

Haydn also showed comparable loyalty to his musicians throughout his tenure as Kapellmeister. He acted as a witness or best man at several of their weddings, and as godfather to many of their children. His close relationship with his players and singers led him to sympathise with their plights, and just before Christmas 1768 he felt it necessary to petition the Prince not to dismiss two members of the Capelle whom he felt were vital to the good standard of musical life at the court. In his letter Haydn referred to growing rumours that the Prince intended to take the entire Capelle to Eszterháza the following year. In addition to protecting the livelihoods of these two musicians, in which he was successful, it seems as if the Kapellmeister was motivated by a desire to establish the truth of these reports. So far, insufficient accommodation at Eszterháza had meant that the entire musical establishment had not been uprooted from Eisenstadt, but Haydn and his musicians must have all felt uncertain about where they would be expected to work once Eszterháza was ready to accommodate the full contingent of court staff. On 24 January 1769 Haydn intervened yet again, to stop Rahier from dismissing a musician for intending to marry a singer colleague without the Prince's permission.

The following summer Prince Nicolaus engaged a theatrical troupe to perform a season of plays at Eszterháza from May to October, and this theatrical activity demanded the participation of the Capelle. The summer season also included the first opera that Haydn directed by another composer: Sacchini's *La contadina in corte*, whilst on 1 August the baryton-infatuated Prince engaged a professional baryton player, Andreas Lidl, who was to remain in the Esterházys' service until May 1774 (he may also have played the cello in the court orchestra). Haydn had apparently made some secret attempts to master the art of baryton playing, often practising late at night, in order to surprise the Prince by performing on the instrument in a concert, but Griesinger recounts that the Prince was rather offended 'that Haydn wanted to usurp his position with regard to that instrument'. Thereafter Haydn never touched the baryton again; but, of course, he continued to write music for it, such as the Baryton Trio in D major (Hob.XI.11).

In early 1770 Prince Nicolaus decided to take the Capelle to Vienna, where Haydn directed a revival of *Lo speziale* at Baron von Sumerau's palace on 21 March. It was around this time that the composer returned to writing string quartets in earnest, perhaps commissioned by Viennese patrons,

Baryton Trios

Haydn composed nearly 200 works for the baryton, all of which seem to have been designed for Prince Nicolaus to play. In particular, there are 122 extant baryton trios, in which the peculiar viol-like instrument was accompanied by a viola and cello. It is believed that five separate partbooks, each containing twenty-four works, were specially bound in red leather and presented to the Prince. At first these works were relatively simple, but Haydn's music grew more technically demanding and complex as Prince Nicolaus's ability on the instrument advanced. None of Haydn's compositions for the baryton were circulated beyond the Esterházy court. By the late 1770s Prince Nicolaus's fervent enthusiasm for the instrument diminished as he instead became enraptured by Italian opera.

and rose to new heights with three sets each containing six quartets (Op. 9, Op. 17 and Op. 20). Perhaps Haydn was inclined to accept more freelance work when he became increasingly worried about finances: his wife was allegedly a spendthrift (and their relationship was already severely troubled), and in autumn 1770 he implored Prince Nicolaus to give him an advance of 400 gulden against his salary so he could repay a debt he had incurred when raising the money to buy his house. It is not surprising that by the end of the year the exhausted Haydn was seriously ill with a raging fever. Griesinger relates that Haydn's doctor forbade him to undertake any musical work during his slow recovery, but that he could not resist composing a piano sonata the moment his wife and maid left the house. On 6 January 1771 Prince Nicolaus granted Haydn's request for an advance, but the composer's illness was still serious enough in early

1771 to alarm Michael Haydn, who obtained leave from the Prince-Archbishop of Salzburg to visit his brother. In the event, Joseph made a full recovery, Michael did not need to travel, and the elder Haydn brother possibly composed his second setting of *Salve regina* (Hob.XXIIIb:2, for four solo voices, string orchestra and obbligato organ) in thanks to the Virgin Mary for blessing him with restored health.

Prince Nicolaus had to spend most of 1771 in Vienna, whilst Haydn continued to experiment with string quartets, and also composed his Piano Sonata in C minor (Hob.XVI:20), which marked the peak of a series of 'expressive' sonatas which were progressively experimental, highly personal in tone, and more harmonically complex than his previous keyboard works. By 10 January 1772 it was becoming clear that Haydn and his Capelle were expected to spend more time at Eszterháza, especially when the estates manager Rahier informed them that none of their wives and children were 'allowed to be seen' at Eszterháza (apart from a few notable exceptions, such as the wives of Haydn and Tomasini). Apparently all the musicians agreed to this, but it is easy to imagine that Rahier did not expect this order to be challenged. Nicolaus was pondering whether to downsize his orchestra and reduce the salaries of its members. In the event, this was averted but it was inevitable that the musical organisation was officially divided into the church music contingent at Eisenstadt and a group at Eszterháza that was labelled the 'Cammer Musique'.

On 25 January 1772 Prince Nicolaus engaged a new theatrical troupe for Eszterháza, the Carl Wahr Company, which was to play a significant part in cultural activities at the palace for the next five years. It would perform comedies, Shakespeare, and plays for which Haydn and his musicians provided incidental music. Operatic works were again given in the larger theatre at Eszterháza, and the Prince additionally organised firework displays, masked balls, and ballets using dancers imported from Vienna. But all this splendour and the experience of performing some of the most daring and brilliant symphonies yet created was not adequate compensation for the musicians who had left their normal lives, homes and families behind in Eisenstadt. Although Eszterháza was initially intended as a summer palace, the musicians (and presumably other members of the court) came to discover that the Prince's idea of 'summer' could last ten months, from February to November. Haydn was still working at Eszterháza on 20 November, when he and Maria Anna stood as godparents for their grand-niece at a service in the nearby parish church. This stay at the Hungarian palace had long outlived the summer, and the homesick musicians were desperate to return to their wives. Reluctant to complain openly for fear of losing their jobs or taking a cut in pay, they asked Haydn if he could do anything to help end their extended exile. Haydn was inspired to make their feelings known to Prince Nicolaus in the most diplomatic but transparent fashion by composing the 'Farewell' Symphony (No. 45). Set in the extraordinary key of F sharp minor, the symphony ends with an *Adagio* (instead of a conventional lively conclusion), in which each instrument in turn falls silent. The symphony was soon performed in front of the Prince, and each musician was instructed that when his part finished he should blow out his candle and leave with his instrument under his arm. This poignant pantomime was understood by the Prince, who reputedly remarked, 'If they all leave, then we must leave too'. The next day he gave the order to leave Eszterháza.

The Capelle was back in Eisenstadt by 6 December 1772. This was Prince Nicolaus's nameday, and Haydn rapidly

Ignaz Pleyel

prepared a splendid new mass for that day's chapel service. Perhaps the *Missa Sancti Nicolai* (Hob.XXII:6) was also a timely expression of the musicians' gratitude for their Prince's perceptive response to the 'Farewell' Symphony. Its lilting 6/4 metres, simple folk-like melodies, and top parts moving in parallel thirds also convey pastoral musical imagery appropriate to Advent. In the meantime, the originality of 'particular ideas' in Haydn's instrumental music had attracted the attention of Empress Maria Theresa (although she somewhat naively described Haydn as 'a beginner' when his works had been on sale in Vienna for twenty years already). During 1772 he had also started a five-year period of teaching composition to his talented pupil Ignaz Pleyel.

On 29 April 1773 Haydn received 400 gulden from funds made available by the will of the late Prince Anton. This was the value of a year of his starting salary twelve years earlier, and no doubt the extra money helped to stabilise his finances. Two days later the theatrical season commenced at Eszterháza, during which Carl Wahr's troupe was probably again supplemented by the Capelle. Haydn composed *L'infedeltà delusa*, his first full-scale Italian *opera buffa*, for the nameday of the dowager Princess Maria Anna (Paul Anton's widow) on 26 July. Probably his most popular and successful opera, *L'infedeltà delusa* was a milestone in his career that possibly indicated to Prince Nicolaus that he could trust his Kapellmeister to create brilliant, tender and witty operas. Haydn presented the autograph score to the Prince, who responded with another shower of gold ducats.

On 2 September 1773, the marionette opera house, in which the stage action was performed by puppets, was inaugurated with Haydn's German opera *Philemon und Baucis*. Concluding with a final scene (now lost) presenting an apotheosis of the Habsburg dynasty, this marionette opera was one of the many festive events that occurred during a state visit by Empress Maria Theresa, who, according to legend, remarked after a performance of *L'infedeltà delusa* that to hear a good Italian opera she had to travel to Eszterháza. In addition to providing musical entertainment during the Empress's visit, Haydn claimed that he also shot three hazel-hens that ended up on the imperial dinner plate. When introduced to the Empress by Prince Nicolaus, the composer amused her by modestly reminding her of the thrashing he had received on her orders when a mischievous choirboy at Schönbrunn. The imperial visit to Eszterháza was a triumph for Prince Nicolaus, who rewarded Haydn's part in the proceedings with an exceptionally generous gift of thirty gold ducats.

Towards the end of 1773 Haydn puzzled about how to replace the late Eisenstadt organist Franz Novotni. In early December he auditioned two applicants, but neither was good enough for the post. He proposed that during summers the castle schoolmaster Joseph Dietzl could play the organ, and that he himself would perform the task during winters. The Prince agreed to divide the salary between the two musicians, and this extra appointment as court organist (winters only) made Haydn the third-highest-paid employee of the entire court, after the estates director Rahier and the Prince's physician, earning the equivalent of nearly 1,000 gulden a year.

On 26 February 1774 Haydn published a collection of six keyboard sonatas (Hob.XVI:21–6), all composed during the previous year, and in an elegant *galant* style. His works had been available in manuscript copies in Vienna for two decades, but this was the first authentic publication of printed music by the composer. In mid-March 1774 Prince Nicolaus was in Vienna, but grew suspicious that most of his musicians were absent from Eisenstadt without permission (perhaps he had seen some of them on the street in the imperial city). The previous January Haydn had been given authority for arranging all such issues directly with the Prince, but the Prince wanted Rahier to secretly check that the musicians were not drawing a monthly salary whilst neglecting their basic duties. Haydn yet again intervened on behalf of his Capelle, but one imagines that while the Prince was away there was a fair number of musicians who were playing truant more often than music.

The Eszterháza theatre season in 1774 probably included repertory that Carl Wahr's troupe performed at Pressburg in the flanking winter seasons: Shakespeare's *Othello* and *Macbeth*, and perhaps Gebler's play *Thamos, König von Aegypten* could have been performed, the last of these maybe with Mozart's intense *Sturm und Drang* incidental music performed by the Esterházy orchestra. If so, this would have been one of the first points of contact between Haydn and the precociously talented young genius, although no doubt he must have heard much about the Mozart family from his brother Michael at Salzburg. Haydn provided incidental music for the Wahr company's Eszterháza production of Regnard's *Le Distrait*, and later adapted it for his Symphony No. 60 ('Il distratto'). *L'infedeltà delusa* was revived on 1 July 1774. In August he was in Eisenstadt, but it seems likely that he was back at Eszterháza in time to direct revivals of his operas *Acide*, *La canterina* and *Lo speziale*. We do not know why he needed to return to Eisenstadt, but perhaps he obtained leave to compose the Italian oratorio *Il ritorno di Tobia* for the Viennese Tonkünstler-Societät, a charity founded by the Imperial Kapellmeister Florian Leopold Gassmann in 1771 to support musicians' widows and children.

The premiere of Haydn's ambitious first oratorio was on 2 April 1775, during Lent. Most of the roles were sung by members of his Esterházy Capelle, and Haydn brought in Tomasini to lead the orchestra (which implies that the venture was fully supported by Prince Nicolaus). Haydn was joining an illustrious group of composers by providing the Tonkünstler-Societät's annual oratorio (previous contributors were Gassmann, Hasse and Dittersdorf), and in so doing was able to compose music for massive forces of about 180 musicians. Haydn's oratorio is notably slow-paced, undramatic, and hampered by a Metastasian structure dominated by recitatives and long arias. However, the audience wanted musical excellence rather than theatrical intensity; *Il ritorno di Tobia* was acclaimed as a success, and the Tonkünstler-Societät made an enormous profit of 1,712 gulden (all participants donated their services with no fee).

A review of the first performance published in a Viennese newspaper four days later stated approvingly that Haydn 'displayed his well-known adroitness at its most advantageous. Expression, nature and art were so finely woven in his work… Especially his choruses glowed with a fire that otherwise one only finds in Handel.'

Prince Nicolaus spent the first part of summer visiting his estates in Poland, but he returned to Eszterháza in July 1775 to supervise the opulent entertainments being prepared for Archduke Ferdinand's visit a month later. This was the most flamboyant and elaborate festival Prince Nicolaus ever produced at Eszterháza. In addition to spoken drama, marionette operas, hunting excursions, masked balls, illuminations, and a village market and circus fairground erected in the parkland, Haydn's new opera *L'incontro improvviso* was performed on 29 August. An eyewitness enthused that the opera, set in fashionably exotic Turkey, was extremely funny, and reported that 'the music, as is customary with Haydn, is excellent'.

Chapter 4

'In whose service
I wish to live and die':
Eszterháza, 1776–1790

> If only I could impress on the
> soul of every friend of music...
> how inimitable are Mozart's works...

'In whose service I wish to live and die': Eszterháza, 1776–1790

Haydn's life and work was transformed by Prince Nicolaus Esterházy's decision to commence regular full theatre seasons at Eszterháza in 1776, including stage plays, marionette operas and full-scale Italian operas. With a theatrical entertainment planned for every evening that the Prince was in residence, it is not surprising that the composer found himself in the role of private opera house impresario rather than Kapellmeister. Between 1776 and 1790 he was responsible for composing, altering, copying (with help from copyists), rehearsing and conducting no fewer than eighty-eight different opera productions. Initially spoken drama dominated proceedings, but during the fifteen years of full seasons this trend was reversed. In 1786 alone the Eszterháza company of singers and instrumentalists gave a staggering 125 performances of seventeen different works.

Under such a heavy workload, Haydn could not be expected to perform only his own works. Instead, opera scores by numerous respected composers were bought from copyists in Vienna. The most popular opera composer at Eszterháza was Cimarosa (thirteen different productions), followed by Anfossi, Paisiello and Sarti. Twenty-four other composers were represented at Prince Nicolaus's opera house. In February 1776 Haydn directed Gluck's famous *festa teatrale Orfeo ed Euridice* (perhaps without the parts for trombones and chalumeaux). The next month Dittersdorf's *Il finto pazzo per amore* was performed. Two more operas by Dittersdorf were produced that summer, and also operas by Sacchini and Piccini. Haydn's only new opera that season was *Dido* (now lost), created for the marionette theatre. Seven new singers were engaged, and the addition of clarinets expanded the Esterházy court orchestra to an unprecedented size. Prince Nicolaus even ordered new red and apple-green uniforms for his musicians.

In the early summer of 1776 Haydn was invited to contribute an entry to *Das gelehrte Oesterreich*, a multivolume 'Who's Who' of contemporary Austrian cultural and social life. The editor, Ignaz de Luca, did not approach the composer directly, but went through an intermediary, 'Mademoiselle Leonore', to whom Haydn replied on 6 July 1776. In this famous autobiographical letter, written in the midst of the first full opera season at Eszterháza, he mentioned his relationship with the Esterházy family, 'in whose service I wish to live and die'.

Haydn might have been relatively isolated at Eszterháza (which was two days' journey from Vienna), but his letter shows that he was acutely aware of musical discussion from abroad. He was evidently irked by the brutal criticism he was receiving from reviewers across northern Germany, who considered that his music was capricious, superficial, and betrayed a lack of contrapuntal knowledge. Haydn responded:

> *I have been fortunate enough to please almost all nations except the Berliners... because they are incapable of*

performing some of my works, and are too conceited to take
the trouble to understand them properly.

He included a selective list of what he considered to be his best-received works: *Le pescatrici* (an opera performed in 1770, about a third of which is now lost), *L'infedeltà delusa*, *L'incontro improvviso*, the oratorio *Il ritorno di Tobia*, and his *Stabat mater*. It is curious that he saw no reason to mention symphonies or string quartets, two genres in which he was a respected innovator. Part of the reason for this might have been simple oversight: his activities in both fields had slowed down in the last few years as his operatic duties at Eszterháza intensified. Alternatively, Haydn might have been conscious that the most illustrious composers of the age were respected above all for their achievements in vocal music for the church and theatre.

Eleven days after writing his letter to Mademoiselle Leonore, Haydn's house at Eisenstadt was destroyed by fire again. This was a more serious fire than that of 1768; this time the town hall, Franciscan church and monastery, brewery, parish church and 104 houses were destroyed, and sixteen people killed, in only two hours. Haydn's house was worse affected than eight years before. He was probably in Eszterháza at the time, but Prince Nicolaus once more paid for his house to be rebuilt. This time the repairs were more expensive (450 gulden), and presumably more musical manuscripts disappeared in the flames. Given his bad luck over the house, unpleasant legal feuds with both neighbours, and his prolonged absences from Eisenstadt, it is little wonder that he decided to sell the house two years later.

In 1777 he was again occupied with operatic activity at Eszterháza. The opera season commenced with Gassmann's *L'amore artigiano*, and was followed in early August by

Haydn's new opera *Il mondo della luna* (based on a libretto by Goldoni), performed in celebration of the wedding of Count Nicolaus (the Prince's second son) to Countess Maria Anna von Weissenwolf. Haydn never revived the opera, but reused some of its music in trios for flute, violin and cello (Hob.IV:6–11) and even in the Benedictus of his 'Mariazeller Mass' of 1782 (*Missa Cellensis*, Hob.XXII:8). Two operas by Paisiello were also performed. Little is known about Haydn's activities during the rest of 1777, but it is during the winter at Eisenstadt that he may have composed the *Missa brevis Sancti Joannis de Deo* (Hob.XXII:7), also known as the 'Kleine Orgelsolomesse' ('Little Organ Mass'), for the local chapel of the Barmherzige Brüder.

The startling reduction of concert and chamber music activity in favour of operatic entertainments at the Esterházy court is manifest from the fact that only six 'academies' were given during 1778 (twelve years earlier, Haydn had been instructed that the Capelle should give two every week). Works by Anfossi and Gazzaniga were added to the Eszterháza opera repertory, and five operas were repeated from previous seasons. On 27 October Haydn sold his house in Eisenstadt for 2,000 gulden (500 more than he had paid for it), which must have alleviated financial pressures caused by his wife's spending and debts incurred by refurbishing the house after the fires of 1768 and 1776. It is noteworthy that he no longer wished to invest his capital in property: he registered half of the money with the Prince's bursar, and made arrangements to receive five per cent (fifty gulden) semi-annually. The composer was clearly thinking about his pension: the last of these payments was made on 13 December 1808, just under six months before his death.

Haydn seems not to have composed much during 1778, but legend has it that at around this time he received a

*The Burgtheater in
St Michaelsplatz,
Vienna*

commission from the Vienna Court Opera to compose *La vera costanza*. He was certainly working on its composition in November, when he requested the purchase of twelve-stave manuscript paper in order to compose the finale. If the legend is true, it seems that his only attempt to create an opera for Vienna's Burgtheater was frustrated by opera house inefficiency and political cabals against him, possibly including the adverse influence of Emperor Joseph II, who was not particularly sympathetic to Haydn's music. It is thought that the composer decided he would sooner not have his new opera produced than continue a futile struggle against small-minded yet powerful opposition; he left Vienna, and told Prince Nicolaus the whole story. He had received a new updated contract from the Prince on New Year's Day 1779, which permitted him to accept outside commissions and to arrange for his music to be published. As one might expect from such a supportive patron, the Prince promptly arranged for *La vera costanza* to be produced under the composer's direction at Eszterháza, where it was heard on 25 April 1779.

Operas by Naumann, Franchi and Felici were added to the Eszterháza repertory, but the opera house was gutted in a fire on 18 November 1779. The fire lasted about four and a half hours, spreading from the Chinese ballroom in the palace across to the theatre. Haydn's autograph score of *La vera costanza* was destroyed (he later reconstructed the opera for a revival in 1785), and probably also the orchestral parts of all the symphonies he had composed for the Esterházys during the last eighteen years. However, the Prince was determined not to let the disaster affect his entertainment, and only three days later the opera season continued in the smaller marionette theatre. It was under these makeshift conditions that Haydn's next opera, *L'isola disabitata*, was first performed on 6 December (the Prince's nameday). Regarded by some as the most perfect opera Haydn wrote during the late 1770s, its unusually serious libretto was by Metastasio. This seems to have been the first time the composer set music to a text by his former mentor. He was proud enough of his achievement to send a copy to the illustrious Accademia Filharmonica in Modena, which was so impressed that a few months later it granted him honorary membership and a diploma.

Work promptly started on rebuilding the theatre at Eszterháza, and on 18 December 1779 the ceremony of laying the new foundation stone featured Haydn's new Symphony No. 70 in D major. However, the unavailability of the main theatre did not deter Prince Nicolaus from launching a massive opera season in the marionette theatre on 17 February 1780. The hectic schedule of ninety-three performances included eight operas, among them the first appearance at Eszterháza of an opera by the celebrated Vienna court composer Salieri. There had barely been a break since the end of the previous season. Haydn, also busy preparing piano sonatas for his first collaboration with Viennese music publisher Artaria, must have been overwhelmed. It is little wonder that he did not compose a new opera for the 1780 season, although a revival of *L'isola disabitata*

might have been curtailed by the departure of the company's capable prima donna, Barbara Ripamonti, in April 1780.

On 1 August the new soprano Teresa Amalia Tavecchia was hired, but by the end of the year Haydn's attention was principally devoted to the young Italian mezzo-soprano Luigia Polzelli, who became his mistress (Frau Haydn was also openly adulterous by this time, especially with the court painter Ludwig Guttenbrunn between 1770 and 1772; such amoral open secrets were commonplace in late-eighteenth-century court culture). Luigia Polzelli had joined the company in March 1779 with her older violinist husband. It seems that she possessed limited vocal talent, and Haydn composed only one proper role for her (Silvia in *L'isola disabitata*). However, many of the 'insertion arias' he composed for his productions of operas by other composers were tailor-made for Polzelli's aptitude for playing soubrettes. Her reputed vocal inadequacy was recognised by Prince Nicolaus, who dismissed both Polzellis from his service in December 1780. Haydn interceded on the Polzellis' behalf, no doubt owing to his affair with Luigia. The pair were promptly reinstated, and remained at Eszterháza until 1790. Haydn and Luigia were lovers for eleven years; she believed that Haydn was the father of her second son Antonio, who became a professional musician and joined the Esterházy orchestra in 1803. We do not know if Haydn acknowledged or accepted this, but it is telling that he was fond of both Luigia's sons, taught them music, gave Antonio a job, and, after 1790, regularly wrote to Luigia sending her money, even expressing an intention to marry her. Haydn also left Luigia an annuity of 150 gulden in his will.

The 1781 Eszterháza opera season opened with *La fedeltà premiata* on 25 February. Haydn's inventive score for this *dramma pastorale giocoso* exploited the libretto's mixture of heroic and comic scenes, and it was an appropriately attractive opera with which to inaugurate the rebuilt opera house, where subsequently operas by the popular Anfossi and Paisiello were mixed alongside new repertory by now-forgotten composers Astaritta and Righini. It was around this time that Haydn probably summoned the famous fortepiano builder Anton Walter to repair three keyboard instruments at Eszterháza. Haydn's harpsichord had presumably burned in the fire which destroyed the theatre two years earlier, and it is likely that it was replaced by a fortepiano built by Walter. Henceforth, it seems safe to assume that the composer wrote his keyboard music for fortepiano and played this instrument instead of the harpsichord (which by this time was considered archaic).

By the end of May 1781, Haydn was again corresponding with the Vienna music publisher Artaria, this time about a collection of German Lieder dedicated to Prince Nicolaus's 'darling' (mistress?) Elizabeth Clair. Additionally, he informed Artaria that he had received flattering correspondence from Joseph Le Gros, director of the famous Concert Spirituel in Paris. Haydn proudly confided that the Concert Spirituel's members were

> surprised that I was so singularly successful in my vocal compositions; but I wasn't at all surprised, for they have not yet heard anything. If only they could hear my operetta L'isola disabitata and my most recent opera, La fedeltà premiata, I assure you that no such work has been heard in Paris up to now, nor perhaps in Vienna either; my misfortune is that I live in the country.

Although he continued to be deeply attached to his supportive employer, Haydn clearly recognised that his isolation at Eszterháza was a mixed blessing. He was fast becoming the leading composer in Europe, but was confined for large periods to a remote palace in the Hungarian countryside. However, Prince Nicolaus's obsession with opera meant that Haydn was no longer required to write baryton trios; and after signing a new contract on New Year's Day 1779, he was no longer obliged to compose instrumental music exclusively for the Prince. He instead produced such music for other institutions or commercial music publishers in Vienna, Paris, London and Leipzig (although it is likely that new symphonies and string quartets were also performed for Prince Nicolaus).

By the end of 1781 Haydn was offering manuscript copies of his new Op. 33 string quartets for sale to selected patrons for six ducats, but on 4 January 1782 he was alarmed to discover that his Viennese publisher Artaria intended to rush them into print. The eager company had announced in the newspaper *Wiener Zeitung* as early as 29 December 1781 its version for mass-market consumption at the price of a mere four gulden. Haydn had not yet fulfilled all the private orders for manuscript copies, and he immediately complained to his publisher that this placed him in a dishonourable and damaging position. Sixteen days after threatening to cease doing business with them in future, Haydn wrote to Artaria again in a more conciliatory mood, reflecting that in future both he and his publisher should act with more prudence. By this time he was also cultivating a business relationship with the English music publisher William Forster.

In February 1782 his new Symphony No. 73 ('La Chasse') was probably performed to celebrate Prince Nicolaus's return to Eszterháza from Paris. The Prince's recent trip might have played a part in the choice of French composer Grétry's *Zemira ed Azor* (in an Italian translation) to open the 1782 opera season. Overall, the season included at least ninety performances, including the first appearance of an operatic work by Traetta. In July 1782 Haydn suffered a serious fall and injured his left foot, which resulted in his being placed on a strict diet and housebound for a while; but he found time to write to Artaria in Vienna, promising the publisher some trios for violin, fortepiano and cello. At this time he claimed he needed to compose a new opera for a state visit by the Russian Grand Duke Paul and Emperor Joseph II. The expected visit did not happen, but Haydn's magnificent new comic opera *Orlando paladino* was performed on 6 December 1782 (Prince Nicolaus's nameday). It was also during 1782 that Haydn composed the *Missa Cellensis* ('Mariazellermesse', Hob.XXII:8, his only major church music of the entire decade), and the English concert promoter the Earl of Abingdon made an unsuccessful attempt to lure the composer to London for the 1782–3 season. The completion of three symphonies (Nos 76–8) tailor-made for the London public suggests that Haydn fully expected to travel to England, and rumours were circulated in the Hamburg-based *Magazin der Musik* that he had already gone. However, he stayed in Eszterháza: Prince Nicolaus probably withdrew or withheld his permission for such an extended leave of absence. The British would have to wait for another nine years for a visit from the composer whom they were already describing as 'the Shakespeare of musical composition'.

The composer was corresponding with Artaria again in January 1783, promising to deliver some overdue symphonies and Lieder, and pleading in excuse that he had spent a fortnight in bed with 'severe catarrh' after returning to Eszterháza from Vienna. The opera season continued apace from March, although none of the 105 performances during the 1783 season were of new operas by Haydn (*Orlando paladino* and *La fedeltà premiata* were both revived). On 8 April 1783 he informed Artaria that his work was now delayed by further medical problems, which necessitated the removal of a polyp from his nose (a recurring affliction), but indicated that one of the symphonies in preparation for publication (No. 69 in C) should be nicknamed 'Laudon' (as he spelt the name of the Austrian military hero Ernst Gideon von Loudon) in order to increase sales.

During July 1783, Haydn's canny (if not downright unscrupulous) business dealings led him to offer the Parisian music publisher Boyer the three symphonies composed for his aborted trip to England. He explained that he could not send Boyer any autographs of his music because Prince Nicolaus was entitled to keep all of them, but offered the publisher manuscript copies of symphonies Nos 76–8. A measure of Haydn's self-confidence and financial priorities may be gleaned from his transparent comment: 'my circumstances are such that he who pays the best for my work is the one who receives it'. It was also during 1783 that he wrote his fine Cello Concerto in D major (Hob.VIIb:2) for the Capelle's principal cellist, Anton Kraft.

In the meantime the composer had given a copy of his Op. 33 string quartets to Prince Heinrich of Prussia; on 4 February 1784 he received a letter from the Prince expressing sincere thanks, noting that the quartets gave him 'much pleasure'. By this date Haydn was presumably close to finishing his new opera *Armida*, which was premiered at Eszterháza on 26 February 1784. It is curious that his last opera composed for Prince Nicolaus was his only attempt during this period at the more elevated and literary style of *opera seria*, although its anonymous libretto, derived from Tasso's *Gerusalemme liberata*, possesses a far greater element of magic and spectacle than Metastasian dramas centring on the concept of noble kingship. Haydn's opera superbly illustrates a wide range of shifting emotions caused by a turbulent relationship between a Christian crusader and an infidel sorceress. On 1 March the composer excitedly reported to Artaria: 'I am told that this is my best work up to now.' It is not known why he then abandoned the composition of his own operas after nearly two decades of intensively working in a genre that he enjoyed; over the next six years he confined his operatic creativity to composing around twenty insertion arias for operas by other composers (which he also adapted and re-orchestrated, as circumstances demanded).

The long Eszterháza opera season included 104 performances of many different operas, generally reflecting Prince Nicolaus's preference for comic operas. Between 22 and 29 March Haydn took a short break in the hectic opera schedule, and went to Vienna to rehearse and prepare a newly revised version of *Il ritorno di Tobia* for the Tonkünstler-Societät. The cast of soloists included several excellent singers who had strong connections with Mozart: soprano Catharina Cavalieri and tenor Valentin Adamberger had created the principal roles in Mozart's *Die Entführung aus dem Serail*, and two of Haydn's other soloists would feature prominently in the premiere of *Le nozze di Figaro*: soprano Nancy Storace (the first Susanna) and baritone Stefano Mandini (the first Count Almaviva).

Haydn's fame was now spreading far across Europe. At about the same time as he revised *Il ritorno di Tobia* for Vienna, the original version of the score was performed at Lisbon on 19 March 1784. Another contact with the Iberian peninsula had developed by 5 April 1784, when he informed Artaria that he was busy working on short string quartets intended for Spain. After his return to Eszterháza, Haydn was visited by the opera composer Giuseppe Sarti, whose works were frequently produced in Prince Nicolaus's opera house; Sarti possibly heard one of his own operas conducted by Haydn in mid-June. The castle and estate that Prince Nicolaus had created in the Hungarian wilderness were now finally completed, and an especially extravagant festival on 12 September celebrated the forthcoming wedding of Princess Marie Hermenegild to Count Nicolaus (the Prince's grandson); Haydn dedicated three new piano sonatas (Hob. XVI:40–2) to the Princess as a wedding gift. In later life she would be a loyal and affectionate patron of the composer.

Correspondence between Haydn and Prince Nicolaus dating from early October 1784 reveals that the Kapellmeister cultivated a garden with fruit trees near some wooden huts on the Eszterháza estate, at entirely his own expense. By the end of the month he had offered three new symphonies (Nos 79–81) to the publisher Nadermann in Paris for fifteen ducats, advertising the fact that his scores were 'very diligently composed and neatly and correctly copied'. In the event, these symphonies were not published in Paris, but instead sold to Torricella in Vienna, and to Forster in London (with the exception of No. 79). However, his contact with Parisian musicians soon led to a special commission from Count d'Ogny, on behalf of the Concert de la Loge Olympique, for six symphonies (Nos 82–7). These took Haydn some time to compose; they were probably finished some time in 1786 and might have been first performed in 1787. They were created for a much larger orchestra than any of his previous symphonies, with about seventy strings and double woodwind. The notably grand style of Haydn's music led to the 'Paris' symphonies becoming very popular – including

'The Hen' (No. 83 in G minor), in which Haydn demonstrates his inimitable humour by ending a minor-key symphony with a merry dance.

Haydn and Mozart

It is possible that Mozart and Haydn both attended a German-language performance of Haydn's *La fedeltà premiata*, which was produced at the Kärntnertortheater by Emanuel Schikaneder's theatrical troupe on 18 December 1784. It is not known when the two composers first met, but it could have been a year earlier at the Tonkünstler-Societät's annual Christmas charity concerts (22 and 23 December 1783), in which music by both composers was performed. They had certainly been aware of each other's music and reputations for some time, and perhaps had some more personal knowledge of each other through Mozart's friendship with Michael Haydn in Salzburg. The Irish singer Michael Kelly (for whom Mozart later wrote the role of Don Basilio in *Le nozze di Figaro*) attended a party given by Stephen Storace sometime in 1784 in honour of the recently arrived Paisiello. It seems that other illustrious musicians were present and formed an impromptu string quartet that Kelly later joked was 'tolerable':

> *There was a little science among them which I dare say will be acknowledged when I name them: The First Violin – Haydn; Second Violin – Baron Dittersdorf; Violoncello – Vanhall; Tenor* [i.e. viola] *– Mozart... a greater treat, or a more remarkable one, cannot be imagined.*

The friendship between Haydn and Mozart could also have strengthened through their interest in freemasonry. On 29 December 1784 Haydn applied to join the masonic lodge 'Zur wahren Eintracht', a group of intellectuals where artists and enlightened reformist aristocrats (including Prince Nicolaus) mingled freely under the leadership of Ignaz von Born (whose lodge included about 200 members). Mozart had recently been advanced to the second grade of lodge membership, and was present at the masonic ceremony on 28 January 1785 at which it was expected Haydn would be initiated. In the event, Haydn was unable to attend: he had returned to Eszterháza at short notice, presumably to oversee advance preparations for the new opera season. Although it is possible that he was not particularly dedicated to freemasonry, his initiation took place two weeks later, on 11 February 1785, when, ironically, Mozart could not attend because he was performing the first of six weekly concerts at a casino on the Neuer Markt. But the following evening Mozart gave a quartet party in honour of his new masonic brother, at which three new quartets were played that Mozart had composed as a special tribute to Haydn. Leopold Mozart, visiting from Salzburg, reported:

> *Haydn said to me: 'Before God and as an honest man I tell you that your son is the greatest composer known to me either in person or by reputation. He has taste, and, what is more, the most profound knowledge of composition.'*

Mozart fully reciprocated this appreciation. Having admired Haydn's Op. 33 quartets, the younger man had been stimulated enough to devote nearly three years to carefully composing six exquisite string quartets that he dedicated to Haydn. Mozart's 'Haydn' quartets were published by Artaria, who, ironically, paid the composer a higher fee than they normally gave to Haydn for such collections. Mozart's lengthy dedication (in Italian), written on 1 September 1785, reveals affectionate respect for his 'dear friend', and compares his 'Haydn' quartets to six children whom he now dutifully places under 'the protection and guidance of a very celebrated man':

May it therefore please you to receive them kindly and to be their Father, Guide and Friend! From this moment I resign to you all my rights in them, begging you however to look indulgently upon the defects which the partiality of a Father's eye may have concealed from me.

Autograph manuscript of one of Mozart's 'Haydn' quartets

Some scholars have regarded the deferential tone of Mozart's dedication to Haydn with suspicion, but Mozart's first biographer Niemetscheck claimed in 1798 that the young Salzburger often called Haydn his teacher, and added that Mozart could be 'moved to tears during the performance of good music... composed by the two great Haydns'. Niemetscheck, who dedicated his biography to Haydn, also reports:

[He] was always very touched when he spoke of the two Haydns... We would not have suspected that we were listening to the almighty Mozart, but rather to one of their enthusiastic pupils.

The late 1780s

1785 was another busy year for Haydn. Although he composed no more new operas for Eszterháza, he was still involved from April to November with eighty-nine performances of repertoire by Sarti, Zingarelli, Anfossi, Stabinger and

67

Bologna. He also reconstructed and revived *La vera costanza* (the original score had perished in the fire), and *Armida* was performed again. Meanwhile, his operas gained popularity away from Eszterháza: *L'isola disabitata* was performed on 19 March 1785 at the Burgtheater in Vienna, and in early June *La fedeltà premiata* was performed at Pressburg. Remarkable visitors began to make a pilgrimage to Eszterháza especially to see Haydn: he was visited by the Venezuelan revolutionist General Francisco de Miranda (a friend of George Washington) in October 1785. Their conversation centred on a mutual enthusiasm for Boccherini's music.

Haydn was taking the accuracy of his published music very seriously. On 26 November he asked Artaria to send proofs of his new piano trios (Hob.XV:6–8); when he received these he was astonished by the bad engraving. On 10 December he wrote to Artaria that he was considering whether to return his fee and sell the trios to the publisher Hummel in Berlin instead, but matters were resolved amicably when Artaria re-engraved the sonatas more accurately.

The 1786 opera season at Eszterháza was the biggest ever held: 125 performances were given between 1 March and 21 December. Amidst this heavy workload it is not surprising that little specific information is known about Haydn's other activities that year. An undated contract with William Forster in London was made in 1786, in which the composer committed himself to providing Forster with twenty symphonies, sonatas, and miscellaneous other pieces. Somehow he found time to compose insertion arias for the revivals of operas by other composers produced at Eszterháza, complete his 'Paris' symphonies, and write five concertos for King Ferdinand IV of Naples for *lira organizzata* (a sort of hurdy-gurdy). It was also about this time that he fulfilled an unusual commission from Cádiz for a series of orchestral pieces based on the last seven sentences spoken by Christ during the Crucifixion (*The Seven Last Words*). These were intended for performance on Good Friday in a darkened church. Haydn devised seven 'sonatas', lasting about seven or eight minutes each, flanked by an Introduction and a concluding 'Earthquake' ('Il terremoto'). He hoped that it would create 'the most profound impression on even the most inexperienced listener', and seems to have succeeded. His Spanish commission spawned a string quartet arrangement, a keyboard reduction and, a decade later, a full-scale oratorio version.

Haydn spent Christmas 1786 in Graz, perhaps visiting his former Esterházy oboist Carl Chorus. By the end of January 1787 he was in Vienna, where an unknown correspondent reported to Cramer's *Magazin der Musik* that he had heard three of Haydn's new symphonies composed for Paris. On 11 February the composer reported to Artaria that he had completed four string quartet arrangements of movements from *The Seven Last Words*, and three days later sent further instructions from Eszterháza for the engraving of the work, specifying that quotations from Christ on the cross should preface each sonata. He signed off with a frustrated comment that his independent work was being held back by rehearsals for the forthcoming Eszterháza season (which featured ninety-eight opera performances).

On 26 March 1787 there was a performance of *The Seven Last Words* at the Palais Auersperg in the Josephstadt suburb of Vienna. Haydn was sufficiently confident of his new masterpiece and his 'Paris' symphonies that on 8 April he wrote to William Forster to negotiate their publication in London. Correspondence on this topic continued for several months. Forster and the London-based violinist Wilhelm Cramer launched an attempt to bring Haydn to England, but the composer instead pondered accepting an invitation to visit King Ferdinand at Naples. He also sent the 'Paris' symphonies to Friedrich Wilhelm II of Prussia, to which the delighted king responded with a personal letter to Eszterháza (dated 21 April 1787) accompanied by the gift of a ring. Haydn reciprocated by instructing Artaria to dedicate the printed edition of his new Op. 50 string quartets (which included the adventurous and highly chromatic quartet nicknamed 'The Frog', Op. 50 No. 6) to the Prussian king:

I feel deeply in His Majesty's debt because of this present, and for my part I can think of no better and more fitting way to show my thankfulness to His Majesty (and also in the eyes of the whole world) than by dedicating these 6 quartets to him; but you won't be satisfied with that, because you will want to dedicate the works yourself, and to someone else. But to make amends for this loss, I promise to give you other pieces free of charge.

On 19 July 1787 Haydn wrote to the London opera impresario John Gallini offering to write a new opera and to assist at concerts in Hanover Square, but, yet again, nothing came of these ongoing discussions to bring Haydn to London. His correspondence from this period often has a mercenary tone, but he was making the most of the liberty he was granted from Prince Nicolaus Esterházy to sell his music across Europe; he often offered the same pieces to publishers in Vienna, London and Berlin. His determination to earn proper recompense for his work was understandable, and our sympathy for his Machiavellian dealings with publishers increases when we read a description of his modest circumstances written by Gaetano Bartolozzi, son of a famous London-based engraver, who visited Eszterháza in 1787:

A musician, it would seem, has as little honour in his own country as a prophet, and of this the celebrated Haydn furnishes remarkable proof... [Haydn's] only reward is a pittance which the most obscure fiddler in London would disdain to accept, together with a miserable apartment in the barracks, in which are his bed and an old spinet, or clavichord.

During 1787 Haydn composed two impressive new symphonies (No. 88 in G major and No. 89 in F major). No longer writing operas for Eszterháza, by the end of the year he received an invitation from Franz Roth in Prague to send an *opera buffa*. Although willing to send one of his comic operas for Roth's personal use, he wrote that he could not comply with the request if Roth intended to produce it on the stage because 'all my operas are far too closely connected with our personal circle [at Eszterháza], and moreover they would not produce the proper effect, which I calculated in accordance with the locality'. Haydn commented that he would be happy to compose a brand-new opera for Prague, but added:

even then I should be risking a good deal, for scarcely any man can brook comparison with the great Mozart. If I could only impress on the soul of every friend of music, and on high personages in particular, how inimitable are Mozart's works, how profound, how musically intelligent, how extraordinarily sensitive!... Prague should hold him fast – but should reward him, too: for without this, the history of great geniuses is sad indeed...

Haydn's letter to Roth gives an insight into his feelings about his own operas, and how he tailored them specifically for the cast at his disposal. But it also illustrates that he was prepared to lose a commission in order to promote his younger friend Mozart, whose fortunes were often mixed. Haydn was granted an opportunity to support Mozart's operatic ventures when he was given special leave of absence in May 1788 to hear *Don Giovanni* in Vienna (Mozart's dark comic opera had been first produced in Prague in October 1787). Legend has it that after the first performance Haydn attended a party given by Prince Razumovsky, at which fashionable connoisseurs took turns to criticise the work of Mozart (who was not present). When, at last, they asked the modest Haydn his opinion, he is said to have silenced the critics with his response: 'I cannot settle the argument. But one thing I know – Mozart is the greatest composer that the world now has.'

The 1788 Eszterháza opera season consisted of 108 performances given throughout the year, including operas by Cimarosa, Sarti, Fabrizi, Prati, Bertoni, Paisiello, Bianchi, Anfossi, Guglielmi and Bologna. Haydn's *Armida* was performed four times. The season commenced on 2 February, and the next day the composer wrote a letter to an agent working for the Prince of Oettingen regretfully postponing the composition of three new symphonies for the German prince. Haydn explained that he was busy writing six *notturni* for King Ferdinand of Naples and a new opera for Eszterháza (the latter claim was a lie; he composed no operas for Prince Nicolaus after 1784). It is obvious that he was prepared to make whatever excuses he thought would do the trick. His unscrupulous business dealings are also evident in his correspondence dating from February 1788. In the middle of that month he wrote to Artaria thanking his publisher for sending him a gift of 'excellent cheese' and sausages, and added a request that Artaria send him the late C.P.E. Bach's last two keyboard works. But on 28 February Haydn was having to defuse a disagreeable situation between rival London publishers Forster and Longman, who both published ostensibly authorised editions of new works in direct competition with each other. The composer was perfectly prepared to blame the confusion on the 'usurious practices' of Artaria, and told Forster that Artaria would never have any more music from him. Only three months later he protested his undying loyalty and friendship to the Viennese publisher ('I would be unjust and ungrateful if I were to throw away your friendship so boorishly'), and on 10 August he emphatically told Artaria that 'it will always be a pleasure to supply you with my works'. At least he kept his word this time; by the end of 1788 he was writing piano sonatas especially for his long-suffering publisher.

During the 1789 Eszterháza season (from the end of February until the Prince's nameday on 6 December) none of Haydn's own operas was revived, although he conducted ninety-two performances of operas by other composers. During this season a score and vocal parts for Mozart's *Le nozze di Figaro* arrived at Eisenstadt. Haydn evidently wanted to prepare his own production of Mozart's masterpiece at Eszterháza the following season. On 8 March Haydn wrote to Artaria that one of his rare, cherished visits to Vienna had been abruptly cut short by Prince Nicolaus, who hated the imperial city and returned with his retinue to Eszterháza. On the composer's return to the countryside he fell ill with 'a violent catarrh' and was unable to work for three weeks. But by the end of March 1789 he had composed his Capriccio in C (Hob.XVII:4) during some 'leisure hours'. He claimed that this fantasia for piano solo would not fail to be well received owing to its 'taste, singularity and careful execution'. He was so confident in this single long piece that he set the price from Artaria at twenty-four ducats, and would not accept a single kreutzer less.

Most of Haydn's compositional activity was no longer undertaken for his princely patron, although it is likely that his new compositions were often tested in performance at Eszterháza. Prince Nicolaus's continuing loyalty to his Kapellmeister is evident in a decree dated 4 April 1789 that Haydn should receive one pig in addition to the terms of his contract. The next day the composer sent the Leipzig publisher Breitkopf & Härtel a copy of his new Piano Sonata in C (Hob.XVI:48), and wrote that he was 'simply overloaded with work'. Part of this workload was a letter to Paris written the same day to sort out yet another unauthorised sale of his music between publishers.

His Piano Sonata in E flat, Hob.XVI:49 was composed for his close friend Maria Anna von Genzinger, a talented amateur pianist whose husband was Prince Nicolaus's physician (and whom Empress Maria Theresa had esteemed so highly that she had raised him to the nobility in 1780). The earliest surviving correspondence between Haydn and Maria Anna, who was able to read full orchestral scores and transcribe them for piano, is dated 10 June 1789, when she sent him her piano arrangement of an *Andante* from one of his orchestral compositions. She confessed that she had prepared it without any help from her music teacher, asking him to correct it and expressing her entire family's affection for him (she had five children). Four days later he wrote to express his warm admiration for Maria Anna's 'excellent' arrangement, declaring that it was 'correct enough to be engraved by any publisher'. Their friendship intensified. Haydn recommended that she purchase a new square piano to replace her old harpsichord, and kindly advised her daughter Josepha about how to sing his cantata *Arianna a Naxos* (Hob.XXVIb:2). Probably composed in 1789 for the Venetian singer Bianca Sacchetti, it is a melodramatic piece for keyboard and soprano voice in which Ariadne, abandoned by Theseus, laments her fate in music that ranges from the doleful to the violent. Haydn developed a tender correspondence with Maria Anna, although there is no evidence that their relationship was anything other than platonic.

The French Revolution, which began during July 1789, did not have much impact on Haydn at first. Only a few weeks after the storming of the Bastille, he was writing to the Parisian publisher Jean-Georges Sieber offering him four symphonies. In mid-October he sent three symphonies to the Prince of Oettingen, about eighteen months after he had been offered their commission, and in his accompanying letter he observed that Prince Nicolaus, even at an advanced age, still had an insatiable appetite for music. But the fifty-seven-year-old Haydn's life at Eszterháza was not luxurious: in early November he reportedly traded one of his string quartets with the visiting English music publisher John Bland in return for some new razors (perhaps this was Op. 55 No. 2 in F minor, but the publisher also struck a bargain to buy the composer's forthcoming new Op. 64 string quartets). The 'dreary solitude' of life at Eszterháza can be inferred from his letter to Maria Anna von Genzinger, written on 9 February 1790 after returning from a stay in Vienna during which he had attended a rehearsal of Mozart's new opera *Così fan tutte* on 21 January:

> *Well, here I sit in my wilderness; forsaken; like a poor waif, almost without human society, melancholy, full of the memories of past glorious days – yes! past, alas! And who can tell me if those happy hours will return again? Those wonderful evenings where the whole circle is one heart, one soul – all those beautiful musical evenings which can only be remembered and not described? Where are all those inspired moments? All gone – and gone forever.*

He confided in Maria Anna that:

For three days I didn't know if I was Kapellmeister or 'Kapellservant'. Nothing could console me, my whole house was in confusion; my pianoforte, which I formerly loved, was perverse and disobedient, and irritated rather than calmed me. I slept only a little, and even my dreams persecuted me; and then, just when I was happily dreaming that I was listening to Le nozze di Figaro, *the blustering north wind woke me and almost blew my nightcap off my head. I lost twenty pounds in weight in three days, for the good Viennese food I had in me disappeared on the journey; Alas! alas! I thought to myself when I was forced to eat a slice of 50-year-old cow instead of your admirable beef... Here in Eszterháza no one asks me: 'Would you like some chocolate, with milk or without? Will you take coffee with or without cream? What may I offer you, my dear Haydn, would you like a vanilla or a strawberry ice?' If only I had a piece of good Parmesan cheese, particularly in Lent, to enable me to swallow more easily the black puddings!*

A few days later Haydn commenced his 1790 season of opera performances at Eszterháza. But Austrian society was about to undergo massive change. On 20 February Emperor Joseph II died, and was succeeded by his brother Leopold. Five days later, whilst Austrians mourned their late Emperor, Prince Nicolaus's wife Maria Elisabeth died at Eisenstadt. It is likely that Haydn hurriedly prepared a solemn setting of the Requiem text *Libera me, Domine* (Hob.XXIIb:1) for the funeral. On 14 March he reported to Maria Anna von Genzinger that he was having to do many things 'for my most gracious Prince in his present melancholy condition'. He observed that 'the death of his wife so crushed the Prince that we had to use every means in our power to pull His Highness out of his depression.'

Haydn's efforts to help the mourning Prince Nicolaus – a token of the composer's genuine affection for his patron of twenty-eight years – were to little long-term avail. The Eszterháza opera season was curtailed when the seventy-five-year-old Prince fell seriously ill during preparations for a production of *Le nozze di Figaro* (August 1790). In order to receive better medical care, the Prince was taken to the Esterházy palace in Vienna, where he died on 28 September. Few partnerships of musical genius and aristocratic patron have ever had such longevity; the death of 'Nicolaus the Magnificent' was the catalyst for dramatic change in Haydn's life.

Chapter 5

Haydn in England,
1791–1795

Haydn in England, 1791–1795

The new head of the Esterházy family, Prince Anton, was not uncultured or unnecessarily stingy, but he did not share his father's obsession with music and the astronomically expensive palace at Eszterháza. Before his accession to power, Anton had already formulated a plan to save money by retrenching the musical and theatrical establishment maintained by his family. Church bells tolled for three days in honour of the late Prince Nicolaus I, who had been both a loyal servant of the Habsburg regime and a supportive employer to Haydn. But during this time of mourning Prince Anton wasted no time in drastically curtailing Haydn's orchestra. The windband (Feldharmonie) was retained for ceremonial occasions, and Haydn and Tomasini were both retained on a salary of 400 gulden but allowed to accept engagements elsewhere. Prince Nicolaus had ensured in his will that his faithful Kapellmeister would be provided for, endowing him with an annual pension of 1,000 gulden.

The rest of the large Eszterháza musical establishment and the theatrical troupe were dismissed. Four of the opera singers were engaged at Vienna on a trial basis, and the remainder (including Haydn's long-term mistress Luigia Polzelli) returned to Italy. Many of the orchestral players returned to Vienna. So did Haydn, who left Eszterháza so hastily that many important papers and scores were left behind. One may imagine that many of the musicians were saddened at their change in fortunes, but perhaps glad to be able to escape their elaborate rococo prison in the wilderness. The fortunes of the fabulous summer palace that Prince Nicolaus Esterházy had created and loved sharply declined after his death. His son Anton never visited Eszterháza again after August 1791, preferring to divide his time between Vienna and the palace in Eisenstadt, which he redeveloped. The 'Hungarian Versailles' became a glorified warehouse in which the Esterházys deposited unwanted furniture; the opera house was demolished in 1870, and the ornate gardens and park gradually ceased to exist. During World War II the palace was occupied by German officers, but in 1945 the Russian army turned it into a field hospital, and brutally destroyed all the remaining furniture, musical instruments that Haydn would have no doubt known, and paintings (including a portrait of the composer in his blue and gold uniform) in a massive bonfire. The shell of the house was left intact, and has been gradually restored since the 1950s.

Upon his return to Vienna in October 1790, Haydn took rooms with Johann Nepomuk Hamberger, a government official who lived on the Wasserkunst-Bastei (near the Seilerstätte), whom Haydn described as a man of 'tall stature', and referred to as 'my wife's landlord'. It was probably in these rooms that Haydn composed some more *notturni* for King Ferdinand IV of Naples and finished the Op. 64 string quartets. Haydn was comfortably off, thanks to his pension from Prince Nicolaus's will and annual salary from Prince Anton; but he was in a position to take stock of his career and accept invitations to travel. Although his music was popular in Paris, the French Revolution made a trip to France untenable. The King of Naples was an enthusiastic admirer of his music, and there had probably been tentative plans for Haydn to visit Italy, where he would have the opportunity to make his reputation as an opera composer. The Prince of Oettingen, an avid collector of Haydn's music, offered him a standing invitation to visit him in Central Germany. Prince Grassalkovics (the late Prince Nicolaus's son-in-law) offered Haydn a full-time position at Pressburg, but the composer politely refused out of loyalty to Prince Anton Esterházy, for whom he was still technically Kapellmeister.

For nearly a decade Haydn had been receiving invitations from numerous entrepreneurs, impresarios and promoters to travel to England. London had an unrivalled public concert life in which many German-speaking musicians played a vital part. Haydn's music had become increasingly popular in London during the 1780s, with a particular impetus provided by the inclusion of Symphony No. 53 ('L'Impériale') in the 1781 London concert season organised by Johann Christian Bach and Carl Friedrich Abel. After J.C. Bach's death, Abel's attempts to continue the concert seasons alone failed, and in July 1782 the concert season was taken over by Willoughby Bertie, the Fourth Earl of Abingdon. Bertie even announced that Haydn was engaged for the twelve concerts to be held during the 1782–3 season, although this plan did not come to fruition. London newspapers continued to speculate that Haydn would soon be coming to England, and his music became popular in venues as diverse as Vauxhall Gardens and the Hanover Square Rooms. Disappointed by frequent false rumours that he was coming to London, some ardent English admirers went so far as to suggest in *The Gazetteer & New Daily Advertiser* on 17 January 1785 that some responsible British heroes should kidnap the composer and bring him to England:

This wonderful man, who is the Shakespeare of music, and the triumph of the age in which we live, is doomed to reside in the court of a miserable German Prince, who is at once incapable of rewarding him, and unworthy of the honour. Haydn... is resigned to his condition, and in devoting his life to the rites and ceremonies of the Roman Catholic Church, which he carries even to superstition, is content to live immured in a place little better than a dungeon, subject to the domineering spirit of a petty Lord, and the clamourous temper of a scolding wife. Would it not be an achievement equal to a pilgrimage, for some aspiring youths to rescue him from his fortune and transplant him to Great Britain, the country for which his music seems to be made?

This was ridiculously harsh towards Prince Nicolaus. In fact, the only grain of truth in the sensationalist portrayal of Haydn's plight is the depiction of his wife. Those who endeavoured to bring Haydn to London came to understand that he would not undertake such a long trip because of his unswerving loyalty to Prince Nicolaus, to whom he felt indebted for having twice paid for his house in Eisenstadt to be rebuilt. One of the London promoters determined to engage him, however, was the German-born violinist Johann Peter Salomon, who read about Prince Nicolaus Esterházy's death whilst touring the continent looking for new singers (perhaps on behalf of the famous King's Theatre). Salomon immediately changed all his plans and set off for Vienna with the sole ambition of bringing Haydn back with him to London. Upon arriving in Vienna, Salomon visited the composer at home, and entered with the famous words: 'I am Salomon of London and I have to come to fetch you. Tomorrow we will arrange an *accord*.'

Johann Peter Salomon, Haydn's friend and impresario

The two men swiftly became good friends, and Salomon dissuaded Haydn from going to Naples. It is alleged that the composer promised Salomon that he would follow him to London if Prince Anton gave his approval. Haydn's employer willingly gave his permission for a year's leave of absence, perhaps with some encouragement from the British ambassador General Jerningham. On 8 December 1790 Haydn and Salomon signed an 'accord' for the 1791 season, and Salomon despatched letters to several London newspapers announcing that he had engaged Haydn for his first major subscription concert series at the Hanover Square Rooms. This venue was owned by John Gallini, who was also the artistic manager of the opera company at the King's Theatre; Salomon persuaded Haydn to compose one opera for London, for which the composer was promised £300. Additionally, he was guaranteed £300 for six symphonies (and another £200 for their publication rights), £200 for twenty other compositions to be conducted at his concerts, and £200 profit from a 'benefit' concert.

After tidying up business with his publisher Artaria, paying his respects to the disappointed King of Naples, and arranging for letters of introduction to be written or sent on his behalf that would be helpful in London, Haydn shared a last meal with Mozart. Griesinger describes how on this occasion Mozart teased Haydn about his trip, saying: 'You won't stand it for long and will soon return, for you aren't young any more,' to which Haydn responded: 'But I am still vigorous and in good health'. Mozart also expressed concern that 'Papa' Haydn would cope badly with the trip because he spoke too few languages, to which the older man responded: 'my language is understood all over the whole world!' During this dinner, Salomon, who was also present, took the opportunity to invite Mozart to London when Haydn returned, but this plan was thwarted by Mozart's premature death on 5 December 1791. Haydn departed from Vienna at eight o'clock on the morning of 15 December 1790, on which occasion the biographer Dies claims that Mozart tearfully bade farewell with the premonition: 'We are probably saying our last adieu in this life'. If the legend is true, Mozart most likely assumed that Haydn would not return from his travels.

Haydn and Salomon travelled on the diligence coach to Linz, and then travelled on to Munich (where they met Christian Cannabich, a leading composer of the so-called 'Mannheim School'). They next journeyed to Wallerstein Castle where Haydn visited the Prince of Oettingen and probably conducted a performance of his Symphony No. 92, which he had sent to the Prince some years earlier. They proceeded to Bonn, the birthplace of Salomon, and stayed two nights at the electoral court, where it is alleged that Haydn was surprised to hear a performance of his own music performed at Mass on the Sunday morning. It was during this brief visit that Haydn was introduced to the promising young local composer Ludwig van Beethoven. The travellers reached Calais (via Brussels) on 31 December 1790, where Haydn wrote a short letter to Maria Anna von Genzinger expressing his exhaustion. On New Year's Day, at seven o'clock in the morning, they crossed the sea to England. This was the first time that Haydn had ever seen the sea, and he later wrote: 'I stayed outside on deck during the entire crossing so as to gaze at that great monster the ocean'.

London

On 2 January 1791 Haydn arrived in London. He lived with Salomon at 18 Great Pulteney Street, and was given a composition studio at a music shop across the road which was owned by the famous fortepiano-maker Broadwood. Within days of arriving, Haydn wrote to Maria Anna von Genzinger about his voyage over the sea (owing to calm seas, progress had been slow; it took seven and a half hours to travel twenty-two miles). He also reported that he had visited the Neapolitan and Austrian ambassadors in London, and expressed astonishment that upon arriving late to hear a concert he was presented before the audience and received 'universal applause... I was assured that such honours had not been conferred on anyone for 50 years'. He was then taken to a banquet in his honour. Albeit flattered, he complained that that he was finding it hard to work on his new symphonies with both incessant interruptions from callers and noise from the street:

> My arrival caused a great sensation throughout the whole city, and I went the round of all the newspapers for 3 successive days. Everyone wants to know me... I could dine out every day; but first I must consider my health, and 2nd my work. Except for the nobility, I admit no callers till 2 o'clock in the afternoon.

Little could have prepared him for the rapturous attention he received from the English. Perhaps for the first time in his life, Haydn appreciated how famous and admired his music had become. London was the largest and busiest city in the world, and he wholeheartedly enjoyed cultivating friendships with a diverse cross-section of English society. His surviving

'London' notebooks contain all sorts of observations about aspects of English life (such as a method of preserving milk that he learnt from a naval merchant, a description of oranges arriving from Portugal in mid-November, an attempt to define the meaning of Guy Fawkes night, and the cost of different types of poultry). The notebooks also reveal his attachment to members of both aristocracy and the affluent middle class, from lords and ladies to entertaining characters such as Mr March, an eighty-four-year-old dentist, coach-

maker and wine-seller who had a much younger mistress. *Charles Burney*
George III liked Haydn so much that he tried to persuade the composer to stay permanently in England (much as his great-grandfather George I and grandfather George II had both supported Handel in London), and the Queen offered him a suite at Windsor Castle. Haydn also became friendly with Willoughby Bertie, the Fourth Earl of Abingdon (who had tried to bring him to London nearly a decade earlier), and the Prince of Wales (the future George IV). Salomon was a considerate and efficient guide during the composer's first few weeks in London and ensured that he soon met the famous music historian Charles Burney, who was so impressed that he presented a specially bound copy of his four-volume *General History of Music* to Haydn.

Upon settling in London, Haydn gave priority to the composition of his new opera *L'anima del filosofo* (now usually known by its alternative title *Orfeo ed Euridice*)

whilst Salomon finalised arrangements for the Hanover Square Rooms concerts. Haydn wrote enthusiastically about the new opera project to Prince Anton Esterházy on 8 January 1791, reporting that the role of Orfeo was to be sung by the celebrated tenor Giacomo Davide. However, Haydn's final Italian opera was ill-fated: although it was completed in good time for its scheduled production in March, its performance was prevented because John Gallini failed to secure the necessary licence for the newly rebuilt King's Theatre in time. Perhaps King George's support of the rival opera company at the Pantheon might have had something to do with Gallini's misfortune. It is noteworthy that the frustrated impresario nevertheless kept his part of the bargain with Haydn by depositing his fee of 5,000 gulden at a Viennese bank. In the meantime, the composer was busy appearing as a guest at private concerts, attending public musical events, and teaching music to aristocratic ladies.

Haydn's series of twelve concerts in the spacious hall on the second floor of the Hanover Square Rooms commenced on 11 March 1791. This was slightly later than expected: the season ran from February to May, and included concerts at the Hanover Square Rooms by Salomon and Haydn (on Mondays) and by their rival organisation the Professional Concert (on Fridays). Operas were planned for Tuesdays at the King's Theatre and Saturdays at the Pantheon, and on Wednesdays concerts were given of 'ancient' music at Tottenham Street. Every other Thursday the Academy of Ancient Music performed music by old masters such as Handel, Geminiani, Corelli, Graun and Jomelli at the Freemasons' Hall. Haydn certainly attended the Academy of Ancient Music's concerts, at which he cultivated his friendship with Burney.

The Hanover Square Rooms had opened in 1775, could hold an audience of 800, and reputedly had excellent acoustics. Salomon had announced in *The Public Advertiser* on 15 January that 'Mr Haydn will compose for every Night a New Piece of Music, and direct the execution of it at the Harpsichord'; but, owing to the delay caused by the thwarted opera project, only two new symphonies were written for this season (Nos 95 and 96). It took a little while for Salomon's venture to be successful. The Haydn–Salomon concerts were also delayed by the tenor Davide being contractually forbidden to perform in concerts until he had given his opera debut. Meanwhile, false rumours of Haydn's decline were spread by the jealous Professional Concert organisation, which had attempted to bring him to London a few years earlier and even now continued to happily perform his music. Salomon was presumably disappointed that subscriptions for his concerts with Haydn were lower than expected despite torrential advertising. Nevertheless, the quality of their performances attracted attention, even from the fickle London newspaper critics. After the first Salomon–Haydn concert, the *Morning Chronicle* enthused that there had never been 'a richer musical treat':

> It is not wonderful that to souls capable of being touched by music, HAYDN should be an object of homage, and even of idolatry; for like our own SHAKESPEARE, he moves and governs the passions at his will. His new Grand Overture was pronounced by every scientific ear to be a most wonderful composition... beyond any even of his own productions.

This 'Grand Overture' was probably Haydn's Symphony No. 92 in G major. Others praised the composer's first official public performance in London as 'an exquisite repast'. These impressions were no doubt considerably assisted by the fact that in London he had an exceptionally good orchestra at his disposal, which consisted of about forty players in the 1791 season (about double the number he had been accustomed to at Eszterháza; this figure grew to about sixty in his 1795 London concerts). The Haydn–Salomon concerts were typically mixed programmes, featuring symphonies and smaller instrumental works (such as sonatas) programmed alongside vocal works such as arias and cantatas (sung by celebrated singers such as Davide, or Nancy Storace – Mozart's first Susanna). Works by other composers featured alongside Haydn's music. The composer played fortepiano continuo during these concerts; the mention of 'harpsichord' in newspaper advertisements was a tradition rather than an accurate indication of the instrument. He shared musical direction with Salomon, who played a sixteenth-century Cremonese violin that had belonged to Corelli.

On 14 March 1791 Haydn wrote to Luigia Polzelli in Vienna. Her sister Theresa Negri was singing in London, and through her Haydn sent his erstwhile mistress some money whilst expressing sympathy that her husband was seriously ill in hospital. Four days later Haydn was performing at the Hanover Square Rooms again, and this time the programme included one of his Op. 64 string quartets. By the middle of April Salomon's concerts were becoming more 'numerously attended' (*Morning Chronicle*, 9 April 1791), and *The Diary; or, Woodfall's Register* praised one of Haydn's newly composed 'London' symphonies that 'exhibited all the fire and perfection of his genius'. Haydn's performances in London also included arrangements of several *notturni* that he had composed for the King of Naples, and he spent a day with Burney and some friends playing through *The Seven Last Words*. A new concert aria for the tenor Davide, featuring oboe and bassoon obbligati (now lost), was sung at Haydn's additional benefit concert on Monday 16 May. Although the audience capacity at the Hanover Square Rooms was 800, it was estimated that 1,500 people crowded in. Haydn courteously published an appreciation of his adoring public in the *Morning Chronicle* on 18 May:

> *Mr. Haydn, extremely flattered with his reception in a Country where he has long been ambitious of visiting... should think himself guilty of the greatest ingratitude, if he did not take the earliest possible opportunity of making his most grateful Acknowledgments to the English Public in general... for the zeal which they have manifested at his Concert, which has been supported by such distinguished marks of favour and approbation, as will be remembered by him with infinite delight as long as he lives.*

During the last week of May 1791 Haydn attended a festival of Handel's music performed at Westminster Abbey. From his position in a box near the royal family, he heard the oratorios *Israel in Egypt* and *Messiah*, extracts from *Esther, Saul, Judas Maccabaeus* and *Deborah*, the coronation anthem *Zadok the Priest* and several organ concertos. He had encountered Handel's music already, perhaps at Baron Gottfried van Swieten's Sunday afternoon concerts in Vienna, but was astonished and overwhelmed at hearing them performed on the huge scale increasingly common in England. These colossal performances featured over 1,000 performers (about 950 more than Handel used for his own oratorio performances between 1732 and the late 1750s!). Haydn's friend William Shield later reminisced that although Haydn had long been acquainted with Handel's music, he confessed that he 'never knew half its powers before he heard it'. (Shield responded to this conversation by sending Haydn a copy of Handel's last original oratorio, *Jephtha*, in order for him to study Handel's dramatic recitatives.) Haydn's biographer Giuseppe Carpani claimed that when the composer heard Handel's music:

he was struck as if he had been put back to the beginning of his studies and had known nothing up to that moment. He meditated on every note and drew from those most learned scores the essence of true musical grandeur.

Perhaps it was at about this time that Haydn began to consider the potential offered by the Handelian model of oratorio, with dramatic accompanied recitatives, sublime solo arias and choral splendour.

The last Salomon–Haydn concert of the season was given on 3 June 1791. Despite a worrying start, the twelve concerts had been a triumphant success, and on 8 June the *Oracle* enthused that 'this amusement has had to boast perhaps a taste superior to any of its rivals… Every lover of harmony will wish a renewal next Season.' Under such circumstances of widespread adulation, it was not difficult for Salomon to persuade Haydn to stay for another season. In mid-May the composer had provoked a riot at Oxford when rehearsal commitments prevented him from appearing at a concert in the Holywell Music Room. A few days later he apologised in the local press, adding that:

A view of Westminster Abbey during the Handel Commemoration of 1784

As the University of Oxford, whose great Reputation I heard
abroad, is too great an Object for me not to see before I leave
England, I shall take the earliest Opportunity of paying
it a Visit.

He fulfilled his promise in July 1791, by which time Burney
had arranged with Professor William Hayes to confer an
honorary doctorate on the Austrian visitor. Nearly sixty
years earlier, Handel had reputedly refused a similar offer,
but both great composers graced Oxford audiences with
performances of their music in the university's ceremonial
Sheldonian Theatre, built by Christopher Wren in the late
1660s. A mixed programme on 7 July included Haydn's
popular Symphony No. 92, which during the nineteenth
century gained the nickname 'Oxford'. Haydn accepted his
doctoral degree on 8 July, and was registered as 'Composer
to his Serene Highness the Prince of Esterházy'. The *Public*
Advertiser reported four days later that:

> *...when Haydn appeared, and, grateful for the applause he*
> *received, seized hold of, and displayed, the gown he wore as*
> *a mark of the honour that had in the morning been conferred*
> *on him, the silent emphasis with which he thus expressed his*
> *feelings, met with an unanimous and loud clapping...*

Haydn recorded in his notebook that he had to pay one
and a half guineas for the bells to be rung and another half
guinea for his robe, but the award of a PhD clearly meant a
great deal to him. Afterwards he often referred to himself in
public documents as 'Doktor der Tonkunst'.

By 4 August 1791 he had received a letter from Luigia
Polzelli, informing him that her husband Antonio had died
after his long illness. Haydn responded with sympathy

but protested that he was unable to send her more money at the present time. The letter contains a clear implication that Luigia and Haydn had secretly dreamed of a time when they could both be widowed and thus openly united, but it is notable that Haydn's relationship with his mistress now cooled. One imagines that Haydn had found more engaging and immediate company with his new lover, the attractive widow Rebecca Schroeter. Sixteen years later he showed his biographer Dies some two dozen letters in English from Rebecca Schroeter, and explained that '...she was, though already sixty [sic] years old, still a beautiful and charming woman and I would have married her very easily if I had been free at the time'.

Haydn spent August 1791 as a guest of the wealthy banker Nathaniel Brassey, at his country estate at Hertingfordbury in Hertfordshire. Here, he walked around the countryside, improved his English, and observed the decidedly eccentric behaviour of his host: upon discussing the large discrepancy between Haydn's early hardships and his own privileged life, Brassey alarmed his guest by violently swearing that he wanted to shoot himself because he now realised that he was not really happy with his life of self-indulgence when there was so much poverty and misery in the world.

On 17 September 1791 Haydn confided to Maria Anna von Genzinger that he planned to reside in England for another eight or ten months, and revealed that he enjoyed his freedom from servitude. However, Prince Anton Esterházy had recently written to Haydn expressing a strong objection to his staying away for much longer than originally agreed. He was caught in an awkward position: he had signed a legally binding new contract with Salomon in London, but now feared the loss of his position at Prince Anton's court (without which he would not be financially secure, despite being the most famous composer in Europe). The Prince had wanted an *opera seria* for Eszterháza to celebrate his installation as Governor of Oedenberg in August 1791, but in the event he gave Haydn permission to stay in London and instead hired Joseph Weigl to provide an opera with a cast imported from Vienna.

It was probably during autumn 1791 that the Professional Concert sent six representatives to Haydn in London to offer him a huge fee for defecting to their organisation. He was not tempted, and remained loyal to Salomon and Gallini. Stung by rejection, the Professional Concert slandered him as incapable of composing anything new, and engaged his former pupil Ignaz Pleyel instead. If the Professional Concert intended to whip up bitter rivalry and animosity between the master and pupil, the strategy utterly failed: Pleyel and Haydn remained on friendly terms (they dined together on Christmas Eve, just after Pleyel's arrival in London), and music by each composer featured in both concert series of the ensuing season.

On 24 November Haydn was invited to spend two days as a guest of the newly wed Duke and Duchess of York at their beautiful country estate Oatlands, during which time the Prince of Wales expressed the desire to have the composer's portrait painted by John Hoppner (the painting is now in the Royal Collection). A week later Haydn travelled 100 miles from London to stay for three days with Sir Patrick Blake at Langham. On the way there, he visited Cambridge, and deeply admired its colleges, gardens, bridges, and the ceiling of King's College chapel. After returning to London, he recorded in his notebook on 5 December 1791 that the fog was so thick that he needed to have lights on in his rooms at eleven o'clock in the morning in order to continue composing. He did not yet know that just a few hours earlier Mozart had died. The news reached London on 20 December, and Haydn was deeply shocked. He wrote that day to Maria Anna von Genzinger that 'Posterity will not see such a talent again in 100 years!' While preparing for the forthcoming concert series at the Hanover Square Rooms, Haydn wrote to Mozart's friend and fellow-mason Johann Michael Puchberg that he 'could not believe that Providence would transport so irreplaceable a man to the other world', and advised Puchberg that he had already written to Constanze offering free composition tuition for Mozart's son Carl. Such generosity may also be inferred from Burney's anecdote that when Haydn was asked by a London music-seller if it was worth buying unedited manuscripts being offered for sale by Mozart's widow Constanze, he responded: 'Purchase them by all means. He was a truly great musician. I have often been flattered by my friends with having some genius; but he was much my superior.'

Such modesty was typical of Haydn, but unwarranted. For his second season in London, Haydn composed four magnificent new symphonies (Nos 93, 94, 97 and 98), and a 'symphonie concertante' for violin, cello, oboe and bassoon. On 17 January 1792 he wrote to Maria Anna von Genzinger that he was 'completely exhausted' from having to prepare so much new music, and complained that 'I never in my life wrote so much in one year as I have here during this past one'. His new lover, Rebecca Schroeter, in a letter dated 8 February 1792, expressed concern that Haydn was fatigued by business. However, he was not too busy to charitably arrange a considerable number of Scottish folksongs for the music publisher William Napier, a father of twelve who had been declared bankrupt.

On 13 February an engraved version of Haydn's portrait by Thomas Hardy was published (the original, painted the previous year, is now in the Royal College of Music). By this time Salomon had announced in the London newspapers that his twelve subscription concerts would commence on 17 February, advertising that 'Dr. Haydn, who is engaged for the whole season, will give every night a New Piece of his Composition, and direct the Performance of it at the Piano Forte'. The first Salomon–Haydn concert of the 1792 season included the premiere of Symphony No. 93 in D major, and the following day the *Morning Herald* reported it to be 'a composition of very extraordinary merit' that proved Haydn's genius 'is as vigorous and fertile as ever'.

On 24 February Haydn premiered his new dramatic chorus *The Storm*, which was perhaps a response to rivals seeking to discredit him on the false grounds that he could not write well for voices. He had also encountered allegations that he was a 'poor performer' on the keyboard, which he similarly disproved at his next concert on 2 March: in which his new Symphony No. 98 in B flat major had its premiere, with Haydn performing a short but skilful fortepiano solo in the finale. Samuel Wesley heard this, and later reminisced that Haydn's keyboard playing was 'indisputedly neat and distinct... [and] executed with the utmost Accuracy and Precision'. Haydn also undermined the attempts to manufacture rivalry with Pleyel and the Professional Concert by ensuring that he attended and enthusiastically applauded all his former pupil's concerts.

The Salomon–Haydn concerts were received with wild enthusiasm by the London public, but, at nearly sixty, the composer was suffering under the strain, and on 17 March 1792 he was bled in an effort to improve his health. Six days later he directed the premiere of his Symphony No. 94 in G, nicknamed 'The Surprise' (allegedly by the orchestra's flautist Andrew Ashe). On 24 March the *Morning Herald* reported that the symphony 'was remarkably simple, but

CD 2 ④

website

extended to vast complication, exquisitely modulated, and striking in effect. Critical applause was fervid and abundant.' Anecdotes suggest that Haydn wrote a sudden loud chord in the *Andante* second movement in order to 'wake the ladies'.

By April Haydn and Salomon were discussing whether the composer could stay for the 1793 season, but on 10 April 1792 Haydn felt it prudent to write to Prince Anton Esterházy that he looked forward to returning to 'serve my most gracious Prince and Lord again'. He soon received word that the Prince desired his presence at the coronation festivities for Emperor Franz II at Frankfurt, but in the meantime he worked intensively on his new Symphony No. 97 in C major, often composing for five-hour stretches without a break. Its first performance might have been in his benefit concert on 3 May, from which he earned £350. The last Haydn–Salomon subscription concert of the 1792 season was on 18 May, although three days later Haydn lent his talents to Salomon's own benefit concert. On 22 May 1792 he wrote to Luigia Polzelli, advising her delicately that a position as a singer in London would not be possible for her, and reporting: 'The English want me to stay here, but this is impossible at present because it's absolutely essential for me to go home, in order to put my affairs in proper order'.

Several more concerts were given until the season officially ended on 6 June. The next day, Haydn attended the Anniversary Meeting of the Charity Children in St Paul's Cathedral, at which he heard 4,000 children sing a chant which apparently made him weep 'like a child'. On 14 June he visited Windsor and the famous horse races at nearby Ascot, and on the way back to London called on Dr William Herschel in Slough (the astronomer who discovered Uranus was formerly a professional oboist and a capable composer). During this period Haydn's relationship with

Rebecca Schroeter intensified, which probably caused him to delay his departure from England until the first week of July. On the way to his rendezvous with Prince Anton in Frankfurt, he visited the spa town of Bad Godesberg near Bonn, where he met Beethoven again. Haydn and Beethoven seem to have agreed that the younger brilliant musician should come to Vienna in November to study with Haydn, and that they would then proceed together to London for the 1793 season.

Back in Vienna

Haydn arrived back in Vienna probably on 24 July 1792 and took up his former lodgings with Johann Nepomuk Hamberger. By October Pietro Polzelli (Luigia's son) had arrived in Vienna, where he studied and lived with Haydn. The following month he was joined by Beethoven, who began to study formal musical theory under Haydn's supervision. Beethoven set to work on simple contrapuntal exercises, probably using Fux's treatise *Gradus ad Parnassum* (from which Haydn had learnt many years before). Beethoven later complained that Haydn was always too busy to give proper attention to the exercises he submitted for correction. As H.C. Robbins Landon observed, the relationship was 'as cloudy and troubled as the relationship between Haydn and Mozart was sunny and mutually encouraging'.

On 25 November 1792 Haydn donated twelve 'German dances' and twelve minuets for a charitable masked ball of the Gesellschaft bildender Künstler; the Empress enjoyed them so much that she requested him to make piano arrangements available. As the year drew to a close, Salomon, and London music lovers, expected Haydn to return in time for the 1793 subscription concerts; but the seeds of the

Napoleonic wars were being sown, much of Europe was in political turmoil, and, more immediately, Haydn required an operation on the polyp in his nose. Whether or not this was a genuinely painful affliction or an excuse, he postponed his return to England for another year, which gave him more time to prepare new compositions for his next London adventure. In advance of his next trip he wrote six string quartets (Opp. 71 and 74), his Symphony No. 99, the second and third movements of Symphony No. 100 in G ('Military'), and most of Symphony No. 101 ('The Clock').

Haydn mourned the passing of his close friend and loyal champion Maria Anna von Genzinger, who died on 20 January 1793 (the day before Louis XVI was guillotined in Paris). By 15 March he had recovered his spirits enough to organise performances of several of his 'London' symphonies at the small concert hall in Vienna's Redoutensaal. He spent the summer at Eisenstadt with Beethoven, whom he introduced to the Esterházys. The plan to take Beethoven to London seems to have been abandoned as their relationship became fraught, but Haydn helped the difficult young genius to forge useful connections with patrons: the Esterházys were among Beethoven's first subscribers for his Op. 1 trios. Haydn also took Pietro Polzelli with him to Eisenstadt, where his official duties as Kapellmeister were presumably slight. On 20 June 1793 he wrote to Luigia Polzelli expressing annoyance at her perpetual requests for more money:

> *Remember how much your son... will cost me until such a day as he is able to earn his own daily bread. Remember that I cannot work so hard as I have been able to do in the years past, for I am getting old and my memory is gradually getting less reliable.*

Baron Gottfried
van Swieten

Haydn was also under financial pressure from his estranged wife, who had settled in a little house in the Gumpendorf suburb of Vienna; she had asked him for 2,000 gulden to buy the house so that she could live out her remaining years alone, but he did not oblige until he returned to Vienna and inspected it himself. Attracted to its quiet location and small pretty garden, he bought the house (probably in mid-August 1793) and had a second floor added.

On 23 November Haydn wrote a report of Beethoven's progress to the younger musician's employer the Elector of Cologne, predicting that 'Beethoven will in time fill the position of one of Europe's greatest composers, and I shall be proud to be able to speak of myself as his teacher'. But in the meantime Haydn presumably enjoyed the popularity of his own music in Vienna, including a revised version of *The Storm* (with a German text possibly by Baron Gottfried van Swieten) that he conducted in the Tonkünstler-Societät's Christmas concerts on 22 and 23 December. It was around this time that Baron van Swieten – a devoted admirer of music by Bach and Handel – started to persuade Haydn to consider composing a grand oratorio in the spirit and manner of Handel, and it is likely that Haydn was involved in the performance of an arrangement of Handel's *Alexander's Feast* hosted by Swieten on 28 December 1793. The friendship between composer and connoisseur led to the Baron donating a comfortable travelling coach to Haydn for his long journey back to England.

Return to England

Prince Anton was reluctant to give permission for Haydn to visit London again, and reputedly suggested that Haydn had now acquired enough fame for himself. However, the Kapellmeister reasoned that he needed to fulfil his obligation to Salomon. Prince Anton relented. Haydn made arrangements for Beethoven to transfer his studies to the famous teacher of counterpoint, Johann Georg Albrechtsberger (although the fiery young man was already secretly studying with the composer Johann Schenk), and set off from Vienna on 19 January 1794. Accompanied by his copyist and amanuensis Johann Elssler, Haydn travelled to Calais via Wiesbaden, along the Rhine, and through the Netherlands. They arrived in London on 5 February 1794 and took lodgings at 1 Bury Street (St James's), close to the Hanover Square Rooms and only ten minutes' walk from Rebecca Schroeter's house in Buckingham Gate (which perhaps explains why no correspondence survives between Haydn and his widowed English lover during his second London sojourn).

The Professional Concert had disbanded, so the Haydn–Salomon series was unopposed for at least ten of its twelve subscription concerts. Salomon had already announced in the newspapers that his concert series would take place on Mondays (except during Passion and Easter Week), and would commence on 3 February 1794, with Dr Haydn supplying and conducting new compositions. Owing to the composer's late arrival in London, the opening night of the series was postponed until 10 February; but his new Symphony No. 99 in E flat major was ecstatically received. The *Morning Chronicle* enthused:

> *It is one of the grandest efforts of art we ever witnessed. It abounds with ideas, as new in music as they are grand and impressive; it rouses and affects every emotion of the soul. – It was received with rapturous applause.*

In addition to giving work to musical refugees from France, the gifted violinist Salomon also generously allowed his previous role as virtuoso to be filled by the Italian violinist Giovanni Battista Viotti. The concerts continued to be successful with public and critics alike, but Haydn was presumably upset to receive news that his official employer Prince Anton Esterházy had suddenly died at the age of fifty-six on 22 January 1794, only a few days after the composer had left Vienna. The new head of the noble family was Anton's son, Prince Nicolaus II: an enthusiastic art collector (he owned paintings by Correggio, Raphael and Claude Lorrain), the new Prince wished to redesign the family's main palace at Eisenstadt, and soon expressed a desire to revive the musical establishment.

Meanwhile, in London, Haydn and Salomon were joined by the great bass Ludwig Fischer (for whom Mozart

Portrait of Joseph Haydn by G. Dance, 1794. Said by Haydn to be the best likeness of him

had composed the role of Osmin in *Die Entführung aus dem Serail*), further expanding the extraordinary variety of musical entertainment offered at the Hanover Square Rooms. On 3 March 1794 Haydn's Symphony No. 101 in D ('The Clock') was premiered to another enthusiastic reception. The *Morning Chronicle* eulogised 'the inexhaustible, the wonderful, the sublime Haydn!' Similar adoration greeted the premiere of Symphony No. 100 in G ('Military') on 31 March. This would prove to be the greatest success of the composer's London career. After a repeat performance on 7 April, the *Allegretto* second movement was described by the *Morning Chronicle* as a depiction of 'the hellish roar of war' increasing 'to a climax of horrid sublimity!'

Haydn's music was so popular that it even found its way into concerts by the Academy of Ancient Music at the Freemasons' Hall (although the Academy's temporary director Salomon might have had something to do with sneaking in music by a living composer). On 2 May 1794 Haydn gave his own benefit concert to a crowded audience, and ten days later performed in the last of that season's twelve subscription concerts. For the rest of May he was busy appearing in benefit concerts on behalf of other musicians, and soon became embroiled in composing piano sonatas, trios and songs. On 3 June six new songs (called 'canzonettas') were published in London by Corri, Dussek & Co. A week later Haydn was alarmed to witness a drunken mob's riotous celebrations of a British naval victory over the French fleet.

Haydn found more amiable peace during his travels around England throughout the rest of the year. He visited Hampton Court on 9 July, where he compared the fine gardens to those at Eszterháza, and then proceeded to Portsmouth, where he was fascinated by the wrecked French battleships that had been towed back by the triumphant Admiral Howe. After visiting the Isle of Wight, Haydn admired the cathedral at Winchester. Back in London by 15 July, he enjoyed a guided tour of the Bank of England, and had a near miss with a tiger in the zoo at the Tower of London. At the beginning of August he travelled to the fashionable spa town of Bath, where he stayed with the famous retired castrato Rauzzini (for whom Mozart had composed the motet *Exsultate jubilate*) and was enamoured of the beautiful architecture. On 6 August he went across to the larger city of Bristol, where he liked the drinking water but found the city itself rather dirty. Twenty days later he was a guest of Sir Charles Rich at his estate near Farnham, on which stood the ruins of a monastery; Haydn was sobered by the thought that such estates had once belonged to his beloved Catholic church. On 9 September he visited the Earl of Abingdon's estate near Oxford, where he might have composed the two English-oratorio-style movements of *Mare clausum*. On 13 October he attended a performance of *Hamlet* at Covent Garden, and a month later he travelled to Preston (part of Hitchin, in Hertfordshire), where he presented his host Sir William Aston with two divertimenti for flutes and cello.

Salomon and Haydn had already publicly announced that the composer would stay in London for another season. With Prince Anton dead, maybe there seemed little reason to rush back to Vienna. However, at some point during the middle of 1794 Haydn received a letter from the new head of the Esterházy family: Prince Nicolaus II wrote that he wished to retain his family's long-serving Kapellmeister, and intended to re-instigate the Capelle. Out of loyalty and gratitude to the Esterházys, he decided to return to his duties after his obligations in London were fulfilled, despite his income in London being far greater than any remuneration he had ever known.

However, the 1795 season did not proceed quite as originally intended. Salomon encountered difficulties in sustaining his own independent season at the Hanover Square Rooms, not least the challenge of finding singers and musicians from abroad willing to risk the journey in such turbulent times. Salomon decided to merge his series with the newly organised company known as the Opera Concert, and in January 1795 announced in various newspapers that this augmented group would give nine fortnightly subscription concerts in the concert room that adjoined the King's Theatre on the Haymarket. Haydn was still the principal attraction of the series, but now became one of four resident composers alongside Bianchi, the keyboard virtuoso Clementi, and the renowned opera composer Martín y Soler. To further complicate matters, the experienced composer and editor of Handel's works, Dr Samuel Arnold, was chosen as choirmaster, Wilhelm Cramer (formerly Salomon's rival from the disbanded Professional Concert) was appointed leader of the orchestra, and the overall musical direction was entrusted to Viotti. The orchestra also expanded to about sixty players, comprising about thirty-five strings, twenty-four wind (including flutes, oboes, clarinets, bassoons, trumpets and horns), and kettledrums.

On 1 February 1795, the eve of the concert season, Haydn was invited by the Prince of Wales to a musical party at the Duke of York's home. Most of the royal family was present, and during an interval the composer was formally introduced to King George III. An eyewitness later wrote:

His Majesty said (in English) 'Doctor Haydn, you have written a great deal.' To which Haydn modestly replied, 'Yes, Sire, a great deal more than is good.' To which the King neatly rejoined, 'Oh no, the world contradicts that.'

The Opera Concert's first offering of the 1795 season included the premiere of Haydn's Symphony No. 102 in B flat, but this was nearly blighted by the accidental fall of one of the chandeliers. Luckily nobody was hurt; and, bizarrely, the incident later led to the nickname 'The Miracle' being attached to the wrong symphony (No. 96). On 7 February Haydn's friend Lord Abingdon was not so lucky when a high-profile libel case resulted in a prison sentence of three months. Haydn, coming from a country where the nobility was untouchable, must have found the scandal quite extraordinary.

Owing to the abundance of competent composers working with Salomon in 1795, Haydn no longer needed to produce new material at an intense rate. After performing in oratorios at the King's Theatre, he premiered his next symphony (No. 103, 'Drumroll') on 2 March. *The Sun* reported that 'Haydn's new Overture was much applauded. It is a fine mixture of grandeur and fancy', but there was widespread disappointment that the immensely popular Italian soprano Brigida Giorgi Banti had withdrawn from the concert owing to illness. Haydn offered the London public ample compensation at his benefit concert on 4 May, when the fully recovered Banti performed *Berenice, che fai?* (Hob.XXIVa:10), a new dramatic concert aria that he had composed especially for her renowned cantabile and coloratura. The same occasion was also marked by the first performance of his Symphony No. 104 in D ('London'), on the autograph manuscript of which he proudly noted it was 'The 12th which I have composed in England'. Although Haydn himself remarked that Banti's singing was 'very scanty', reviews of the concert were, as usual, laudatory. The *Morning Chronicle* reported that the symphony was thought 'to surpass all his other compositions'.

CD 2 [5]

website

On 16 May 1795 Haydn was a witness at the wedding of the pianist Therese Jansen and Gaetano Bartolozzi (who had visited Haydn at Eszterháza some years previously), and two days later the Opera Concert gave the last of its nine subscription concerts. Several benefit concerts were given at the end of the season, and Haydn's last known public performance in London was at the benefit concert of the flautist Andrew Ashe on 8 June 1795 in the King's Theatre. He spent another two months quietly working in London, where had cultivated a profitable relationship with several music publishers: during this second stay in England, he composed sonatas, English songs and piano trios (including three dedicated to Prince Anton Esterházy's widow, Maria Therese, and another three dedicated to the new Prince's wife, Marie Hermenegild).

On 13 August Haydn and Salomon signed a contract giving the impresario copyright for the first six 'London' symphonies (a similar agreement was made for the second set six months later), and perhaps it was on this occasion that Salomon gave Haydn a manuscript libretto of an English oratorio called *The Creation*. An anonymous text based on Milton's *Paradise Lost*, it had supposedly been offered to Handel many years before, and he declined to set it to music. On 15 August Haydn left England for the last time. He later reflected that the days spent in England were the happiest of his life; they were certainly his most successful. Having worked almost exclusively for a public audience that nurtured a system in which a composer could earn respectable fees, he earned the equivalent of about 24,000 gulden, and probably returned home to Vienna with a pure profit of 13,000 gulden. This was more than six times the capital he had owned before his first trip to England, and the equivalent of more than twenty years of his normal salary at the Esterházy court. And the works that he had composed for London proved to be his supreme and final masterpieces in both symphonic and operatic genres.

Chapter 6

Vienna, 1795–1809

"You see how the notes run up and down like the waves: see there, too, the mountains that come up from the depths of the sea?"

Vienna, 1795–1809

The blessing of English-granted financial security did not guarantee Haydn and his copyist Elssler an easy trip home. With England now at war with France, they had to take the long sea crossing to Hamburg, where they landed on 20 August. They travelled by stagecoach to Vienna via Berlin and Dresden. The journey probably took about two weeks; by early September 1795 Haydn was ready to resume his post as the Esterházy family's Kapellmeister in the imperial city. The new house he had bought in the Gumpendorf suburb of Vienna in 1793 was still undergoing building work, so he temporarily took lodgings on the Neuer Markt in the centre of the old city.

The new head of the family, Prince Nicolaus II, soon abandoned Eszterháza completely, preferring to spend summers in Eisenstadt and winters at the family's Wallnerstrasse palace in Vienna. Nicolaus II was possibly the most disagreeable of Haydn's four Esterházy employers. Although fond of old-fashioned church music, he was in fact a compulsive gambler, maintained multiple mistresses, and nearly squandered the entire family's fortune that had been so carefully managed by his predecessors. Nicolaus II was initially disrespectful towards Haydn, and soon after Haydn's return from England needed to be reminded that a Doctor of Music from the University of Oxford and the most celebrated living composer in Europe deserved better treatment. Haydn was known for his modesty, but he was not prepared to be insulted, even by his Prince. It was probably in about 1795–6 that Nicolaus II attended one of Haydn's orchestral rehearsals and criticised something, to which the composer publicly responded, 'Your Highness, that is *my* business'. The Prince apparently left the room in fury. However, Princess Marie Hermenegild was more immediately appreciative, and, thanks to her influence, the Prince became more cordial and supportive towards his Kapellmeister.

Although Nicolaus II wished to restore the musical establishment that had been dissolved by his father, he did not expect Haydn to perform onerous duties. Music-making at Eisenstadt was concentrated during the weeks before and after the nameday of Marie Hermenegild (8 September), and it incorporated two resident ensembles: a group of about eight string players employed to provide church music (including Haydn's old friend and long-time colleague Tomasini), and a windband (Feldharmonie) consisting of two oboes, two clarinets, two horns (whose players switched to trumpets when required) and two bassoons. Although the two groups were occasionally combined and slightly expanded, the magnificent orchestra from the reign of Nicolaus I was never reinstated.

Under these circumstances the sixty-three-year-old Haydn was able to focus his musical activities in Vienna for the first time since the 1750s. In the intervening years his relationship with influential individuals and organisations in Vienna had been strained and under-developed, but from 1795 he was embraced as a national hero in the imperial city. The young new Emperor Franz II was, unlike his predecessors, appreciative and supportive of Haydn, and his Empress Marie Therese was the daughter of Haydn's avid fan King Ferdinand of Naples. Where Haydn had once been marginalised by the Italianate tastes of Joseph II and his brother and successor Leopold II, the new imperial couple frequently invited the composer to the Hofburg after he had settled in Vienna. He also cultivated strong links with several important aristocratic patrons, including Johann Joseph Nepomuk, Prince of Schwarzenberg, and the passionate music lover Prince Joseph Franz Lobkowitz, then in his mid-twenties, and later to become a dedicated supporter of Beethoven. Above all, Haydn enjoyed the support of loyal patron and occasional collaborator Baron Gottfried van Swieten. From 1777 until his death, Swieten was Prefect of the Imperial Library at Vienna, where he gave Sunday afternoon concerts. Swieten, albeit a rather stiff and formal person, was an avid collector of music by J.S. Bach and Handel, and in the second half of the 1780s he organised a group of aristocratic patrons known as the Gesellschaft der Associierten to sponsor performances of Handel's oratorios and odes (albeit re-orchestrated by Mozart and others, and in German translations). Haydn was soon to develop strong links with Swieten and his musical association.

In autumn 1795 Haydn visited his birthplace Rohrau, where he was doubtless flattered when shown by the local lord, Count Harrach, a monument erected in his honour in the castle garden. The only new composition Haydn is known to have composed in late 1795 is the Piano Trio in E flat minor (Hob.XV:31), and he understandably gave priority to performing his recent London compositions in Vienna. It is likely that the 'Drumroll' Symphony, No. 103, was performed on 21 September, but Vienna did not have a public musical life comparable to that of London; instead composers would organise their own benefit concert, announce it in the press, and hope the public would come.

Haydn hired the small room at the Redoutensaal for a concert on 18 December 1795, at which three of his 'London' symphonies (including the 'Military', No. 100) previously unheard in Vienna were performed. He generously invited his former pupil Beethoven to take part, and the young firebrand played his Piano Concerto in B flat (Op. 19). The esteemed older composer also probably had a hand in Beethoven's first Viennese orchestral commission (dances and minuets) from the Redoutensaal Masked Ball.

On 8 January 1796 Haydn and Beethoven again performed in the same concert at the Redoutensaal, and Haydn's recent 'London' symphonies began to attract a lot of attention. The music collector Prince Karl Fürstenberg swiftly ordered a complete set of all twelve, and the composer's old patron the Prince of Oettingen eagerly enquired about how to get copies whilst also expressing a desire to commission new symphonies. On 27 February Salomon and Haydn signed an agreement that the second group of six 'London' symphonies were the sole property of the London impresario, with Haydn promising 'to make no other but personal use of them'. 'Personal use' clearly included concert performances in Vienna for either his own benefit or in aid of others, but Salomon now owned the official publication rights to all twelve symphonies. This was only fair: Haydn had been paid good money for his work, and Salomon no doubt deserved some reward for his investment.

Haydn soon embarked on his first oratorio collaboration with Gottfried van Swieten. *The Seven Last Words* was an orchestral work that he had written for Cádiz in 1786, and a year later adapted into a string quartet version. Now inspired by an oratorio-style arrangement by Joseph Friebert that he had heard in Passay, on the way back from London, Haydn reworked Friebert's version by adding chorale-like *a cappella* intonations to precede most movements, rewriting Friebert's choral parts and orchestration, and composing a new windband introduction to the second part. The German libretto text that Friebert had used was revised by Swieten, who arranged for the Gesellschaft der Associierten to subsidise performances at Prince Schwarzenberg's palace on 26 and 27 March 1796. It was Haydn's first 'proper' oratorio since *Il ritorno di Tobia* twenty-one years earlier, and quickly became an established favourite for Lent.

A few days later Haydn's 'Surprise' Symphony was privately performed in Vienna. Another link back to his time in England was also made in August 1796, when he signed a contract with the London music publisher Frederick Augustus Hyde, which had been witnessed in London by Haydn's lover Rebecca Schroeter. Hyde expected that Haydn would supply piano trios and sonatas, and set a presumably hypothetical figure of 'fifty-five compositions' for which the composer would receive a total sum of no more than £911.

Haydn now entered a richly creative period. Although he was not as prolific as he had been during his first London visit, his music composed in the late 1790s was consistently superb. He wrote the Trumpet Concerto in E flat (Hob.VIIe:1) for the Viennese court musician Anton Weidinger, and also produced his last four piano trios. From Easter to September 1796 he wrote the first of his six late masses, most of which were intended to celebrate the nameday of Princess Marie Hermenegild. The *Missa Sancti Bernardi von Offida* ('Heiligmesse', Hob.XXII:10) was first performed at the Bergkirche in Eisenstadt. It was the first mass Haydn had composed since 1782, partly owing to the fact that elaborate church music had been discouraged during the reign of Emperor Joseph II, but mainly because Prince Nicolaus I had demanded that his musical establishment at Eszterháza should concentrate on secular and operatic ventures. Haydn's official duties that autumn also included the composition of three substantial pieces of incidental music for *Alfred, König der Angelsachsen, oder Der patriotische König* (an adaptation of an English play) which was performed at Eisenstadt on 9 September.

While at Eisenstadt it is likely that Haydn conducted a performance of Mozart's *Die Zauberflöte*, and he began work on his next mass, the *Missa in tempore belli* ('Paukenmesse', Hob.XXII:9). Known as the 'Mass in Time of War', it was composed while the war against the advancing French (led by Napoleon) intensified, and was almost certainly commissioned by the Imperial Royal Paymaster Johann Franz von Hofmann. It was first performed in the Piaristenkirche in Vienna on 26 December 1796, as part of a service in which Hofmann's son entered the priesthood. But by this time Haydn's full attention was devoted to his magnum opus: *Die Schöpfung* ('The Creation').

Die Schöpfung ('The Creation')

Eleven days before the *Missa in tempore belli* was premiered, Johann Georg Albrechtsberger had written to Beethoven:

> *Yesterday Haydn came to me, he is carrying round in his head the idea of a big oratorio which he intends to call 'The Creation' and hopes to finish it soon. He improvised some of it for me and I think it will be very good.*

In fact, the English libretto that Salomon had given Haydn before leaving London had already been occupying the composer's thoughts for some time. At some point after returning to Vienna, he had shown Swieten the text, and the Baron – who had a good knowledge of English – offered to prepare an abridged translation in German. Swieten immediately recognised that its exalted subject offered ideal potential for the sort of oratorio he had long desired his friend to write:

> *I therefore encouraged him to take the work in hand, and... resolved to clothe the English poem in German garb... It is true that I followed the plan of the original faithfully as a whole, but I diverged from it in details as often as musical progress and expression... seemed to demand.*

In the autumn of 1796 Haydn made compositional sketches for *The Creation* (in the same manuscript that he had used for the *Missa Sancti Bernardi von Offida*) and continued to concentrate on his new oratorio throughout 1797. At some point the Swieten–Haydn collaboration on *The Creation* became an officially supported commission from the Gesellschaft der Associierten, and plans were initiated to organise a performance at Prince Schwarzenberg's palace in spring 1798. Haydn, no doubt still under the spell cast by his experience of Handel's music in London, had tremendous enthusiasm for the most ambitious work he ever produced. He even conceived the peculiar notion of disseminating the oratorio in both English and German, which made it arguably the first original bilingual composition. Swieten had adapted the original English text into German, and subsequently prepared a new English text that would fit Haydn's musical setting of the German words. Work on the oratorio proceeded slowly, with Swieten freely contributing many ideas and comments at each stage of the creative process.

In the meantime, the Tonkünstler-Societät extended an olive branch to the composer, whom it had thoughtlessly insulted nearly twenty years earlier. In January 1779 it had unrealistically demanded that he should compose new music free of charge whenever it wished him to. Haydn had rightly refused and resigned from the charity, although he continued to support it on an informal and occasional basis. But on 20 January 1797, in a letter signed by Salieri and the charity's secretary Paul Wranizky (a violinist who had studied with Haydn), the Tonkünstler-Societät unreservedly apologised, profoundly thanked Haydn for having donated his profitable services, and sought to make amends by offering Haydn free tickets for all future concerts. During January 1797 Haydn also somehow found time to compose the *Volkslied* for Count Saurau; it was swiftly adopted as the Austrian national anthem, *Gott erhalte Franz den Kaiser*. The following months saw the completion of the Op. 76 set of string quartets (not published until 1799, when they were dedicated to Count Joseph Erdődy), in which the composer made good use of the *Volkslied* as the slow movement of the so-called 'Emperor' Quartet, No. 3.

At the end of March Haydn attended a performance of Handel's *Acis and Galatea* at Prince Schwarzenberg's palace, where he met the Swedish diplomat Frederik Samuel Silverstolpe. Blessed with a remarkable memory for details and conversations, Silverstolpe later recounted that in spring 1797 Haydn was living in a rented house called *Der blaue Säbel* on the Krügerstrasse. Although the composer had technically taken up residence in his own new house in Gumpendorf about a year earlier, it is not surprising that he chose to be both apart from his irritating wife and closer to Swieten whilst they worked together on *The Creation*.

Silverstolpe recalled that on one visit to Haydn's lodgings the composer played him the introduction of the oratorio, designed to portray chaos:

> *He asked me to come and sit beside him, so as to follow the score. When the piece was ended, he said: 'You have certainly noticed how I avoided the resolutions that you would most readily expect. The reason is, that there is no form in the universe yet.'*

A performance of the new oratorio version of *The Seven Last Words* was planned for 7 April 1797, but it was abandoned owing to catastrophic news about Austria's losses against Napoleon's army in Italy. A few days later, preparations began to fortify Vienna against a siege. By summer 1797 Haydn was living in his own house again, and one suspects that his estranged wife spent the summer away at the fashionable spa at Baden. Silverstolpe visited him at Gumpendorf, admired his collection of German poetry, and again found him busy working at the subtleties in his oratorio-in-progress. Showing his visitor the stormy aria 'Rolling in foaming billows' ('Rollend in schäumenden Wellen'), the composer jovially remarked:

> *You see how the notes run up and down like the waves: see there, too, the mountains that come up from the depths of the sea? One has to have some amusement after one has been serious for so long.*

Haydn later told his friend and biographer Griesinger:

> *It was not till I reached the half of my composition that I noticed that it had turned out well; I was also never so devout*

as during that time when I was working on The Creation*;
every day I fell on my knees and asked God to give me the
strength to enable me to pursue the work to its successful
conclusion.*

By autumn 1797 Haydn was at Eisenstadt to play his
part in the Princess's nameday celebrations: on Sunday 10
September a new choral motet was performed (probably
Insanae et vanae curae, an adaptation of the 'storm' chorus
from *Il ritorno di Tobia*), some of the new Op. 76 string
quartets were played on 28 September, and the following
day the recent *Missa in tempore belli* was revived. On 27
October Haydn directed a performance of the oratorio
version of *The Seven Last Words*. Prince Nicolaus II was
pleased enough to raise his Kapellmeister's salary, which
now consisted of his annual pension of 1,000 gulden from
Nicolaus I and another annual payment of 700 gulden. This
no doubt cheered Haydn as he completed his first draft
score of *The Creation* while still in Eisenstadt.

He probably returned to Vienna during November
1797, and on 11 December his full reconciliation with the
Tonkünstler-Societät was completed by his unanimous
election as an honorary member and appointment as
'Assessor senior' for life. In a particularly moving gesture,
Count Johann Esterházy (a distant relative of Haydn's
masters) led Haydn into the Redoutensaal, where the
members of the Tonkünstler-Societät cried 'Vivat!' and
applauded the sixty-five-year-old composer. He attended
his first business meeting at the Tonkünstler-Societät on
10 March 1798, but was otherwise preoccupied during the
first few months of the new year revising *The Creation* and
supervising Elssler's preparation of performance material.
He attended a benefit concert by his godson Joseph Weigl

on 30 March, and on 1 and 2 April conducted *The Seven Last Words*, an apt choice for the Tonkünstler-Societät's Lenten oratorio concerts. The charity received its highest income to date from these concerts, which featured a notably large chorus and orchestra.

On 6 April 1798 Prince Schwarzenberg was informed that everything was now ready for *The Creation* to be performed, and a private premiere was swiftly organised for 30 April at the Prince's palace on the Mehlmarkt (Neuer Markt). Ten members of the Gesellschaft der Associierten pledged fifty ducats each, in order to provide Haydn with a fee of 500 ducats (five times more than Mozart had earned a decade earlier for *Le nozze di Figaro*). An open rehearsal which the public could attend took place on 29 April, at which the three soloists were the twenty-one-year-old soprano Christine Gerardi (who soon married Dr Joseph Frank, the physician and friend of Beethoven), tenor Mathias Rathmayer (an academic and doctor), and the bass Ignaz Saal (whose daughter Therese was soon to become a successful soprano); Salieri played fortepiano continuo, and Haydn conducted.

The audience was astonished by the way in which the birth of light was portrayed through music. Silverstolpe described:

> *That was the only passage of the work which Haydn had kept hidden (even from Baron van Swieten). I think I see his face even now, as this part sounded in the orchestra. Haydn had the expression of someone who is thinking of biting his tongue, either to hide his embarrassment or to conceal a secret. And in that moment when light broke out for the first time, one would have said that rays of light darted from the composer's blazing eyes.*

Silverstolpe remarked that the Viennese public was so electrified by this extraordinary moment that the rehearsal ground to a halt for some minutes; Prince Schwarzenberg was so enchanted with the many beauties of Haydn's new oratorio that he presented the composer with 100 ducats. On the day of the official premiere the Prince had to pay for thirty policemen (most of whom were mounted) to keep order among the crowds assembled outside his palace's entrance. The response from the audience was so overwhelming that repeat performances were produced on 7 and 10 May.

There is no doubt that Haydn appreciated the effusive acclaim showered upon him in the wake of *The Creation*, but it seems he suffered from exhaustion after these performances and was ordered by his doctor to take a rest. He retreated from Vienna to Eisenstadt, where he took a break from work and went on some medicinal trips to the nearby sulphur baths at Schützen am Gebirge. Haydn soon realised that he needed to compose a new mass for Princess Marie Hermenegild Esterházy's nameday celebration service on Sunday 9 September 1798. This was the anniversary of the Austrian victory over the Turkish invaders in 1683, so on 10 July he began work on his dramatic *Missa in angustiis* ('Mass in Straitened Times', Hob.XXII:11; popularly known as the 'Nelson Mass'). Haydn normally took about three months to compose a large-scale mass, but on this occasion managed the task in about half the normal time (he finished and dated his autograph score on 31 August). Unfortunately, it was impossible to prepare the necessary performance material and adequately rehearse in time for the Princess's nameday service, so the *Missa in angustiis* was instead performed a fortnight later on 23 September in the Stadtpfarrkirche. The political and military turmoil

Autograph score of the Kyrie from Haydn's 'Nelson Mass'

spreading across Europe in the late 1790s – and the inauthentic nineteenth-century nickname associating the mass with the English hero Admiral Nelson – has led some to search for a militaristic sentiment behind Haydn's decision to register this as the 'Mass in Straitened Times'. But there is probably an innocent explanation. Prince Nicolaus II had retrenched his musical establishment by unceremoniously firing the Feldharmonie wind octet; Haydn knew he would not have the oboes, clarinets, bassoons and horns that had previously been at his disposal, so he deliberately scored the *Missa in angustiis* for these 'straitened' circumstances; although three trumpeters were hired for the occasion, the mass is otherwise simply scored for solo voices, choir, strings, timpani and organ (which Haydn himself played).

The Esterházy court remained at Eisenstadt until late October 1798, and when Haydn returned to Vienna he was visited by his younger brother Michael, whom he had not seen since the early 1760s. Michael, a respected composer in his own right, had obtained leave from his position at Salzburg, and it is likely that the two Haydns attended a revival of Mozart's *Die Entführung aus dem Serail* and concerts at the Theater auf der Wieden in which Beethoven played a piano concerto. On one of his visits to his brother's house at Gumpendorf, Michael was delighted with an unexpected windband concert in his honour.

It was during 1798 that Franz Xavier Niemetschek's pioneering biography of Mozart was published in Prague. It was dedicated to Haydn, who was addressed as 'Father of the noble art of music and the favourite of the Muses'. The composer was also granted a free subscription to the newly instituted musical journal *Allgemeine musikalische Zeitung*, which Breitkopf & Härtel launched on 3 October 1798. The Tonkünstler-Societät's Christmas concerts on 22 and 23 December 1798 included Haydn's 'Military' Symphony and his new concert aria *Solo e pensoso* (Hob.XXIVb:20, a setting of Petrarch's twenty-eighth sonnet). It was also the first known public performance of Anton Weidinger playing his recently invented keyed trumpet (although he did not yet venture to play in public the concerto that Haydn had composed for him).

On 2 and 4 March 1799 there were two more private performances of *The Creation* at Prince Schwarzenberg's palace. By this time Breitkopf & Härtel was desperate to produce a printed edition of *The Creation*, and unsuccessfully attempted to persuade Mozart's widow Constanze to negotiate a deal with her friend Haydn on its behalf. On 8 March *The Storm* was performed at Prince Lobkowitz's, and on 17 March Haydn conducted the Tonkünstler-Societät's performances of his *Seven Last Words*. A repeat performance was given the next day, on which he also directed a general rehearsal of *The Creation* at noon in readiness for the oratorio's first public performance at the Burgtheater on 19 March 1799 (appropriately, this was St Joseph's Day). About 180 performers were engaged to take part, and Swieten and his Gesellschaft der Associierten met all the performance and venue costs so that the proceeds were donated to the composer.

Announcement of the first public performance of The Creation

Although the concert started at seven o'clock in the evening, crowds had gathered and caused havoc three hours earlier. The theatre was crammed full, but a poster advertising the concert contained a message in which the audience was politely requested not to expect encores of individual movements, 'for otherwise the true connection between the various single parts, from the uninterrupted succession of which should proceed the effect of the whole, would be necessarily disturbed'. One eyewitness wrote in his memoirs that between the sections of the oratorio there was 'tumultous applause', but that during each section 'it was as still as the grave'. A Viennese satirist remarked that when the music began one could have heard a mouse running, but concluded:

> For the life of me I wouldn't have believed that human lungs and sheep gut and calf's skin could create such miracles. The music all by itself described thunder and lightning... you'd have heard the rain falling and the water rushing and even the worms crawling on the ground... I never left a theatre more contented and all night I dreamed of the Creation of the World.

The *Allgemeine musikalische Zeitung* acclaimed the oratorio as 'This masterpiece of the new musical age', and announced that Swieten and Haydn were planning a sequel called *Die Jahreszeiten* ('The Seasons'). Haydn started composing the music for his last oratorio in autumn 1799, but in the meantime he was visited on 25 May by Georg August Griesinger; this young Saxon theologian and music lover became a close friend, and their many conversations together resulted in Griesinger's classic biography of the composer (published only one year after Haydn's death). Griesinger was particularly keen to meet

Haydn in order to negotiate music publications on behalf of Breitkopf & Härtel; he reported back that the great old man could not commit to much because he was busy working on a new *Te Deum* for Empress Marie Therese and a new mass for the Esterházys. Perhaps the Leipzig firm still harboured ambitions to publish the first edition of *The Creation*, but in the event Haydn decided to publish the score independently. On 15 June 1799 he announced to the *Wiener Zeitung* and *Allgemeine musikalische Zeitung*:

> *The success which my oratorio* The Creation *has been fortunate enough to enjoy... induces me to arrange for its dissemination myself. Thus the work will appear... neatly and correctly engraved and printed on good paper, with German and English texts; and in full score, so that [at least] one of my compositions will be available to the general public in its entirety, and the connoisseur will be in a position to judge it as a whole.*

Haydn publicly seemed as prolific and marvellous as ever, but three days earlier he had written a letter to Breitkopf & Härtel which gives an illuminating glimpse of the sixty-seven-year-old composer's gradual decline in energy:

> *Every day the world compliments me on the fire of my recent works, but no one will believe the strain and effort it costs me to produce them. There are some days when my enfeebled memory and... nerves crush me down to such an extent that I suffer from the worst kind of depression, and am afterwards quite unable to find even a single idea for many days...*

The relationship between Haydn and Breitkopf & Härtel became sufficiently warm and positive that in the June issue of *Allgemeine musikalische Zeitung* the publisher announced a 'tasteful and exceptionally inexpensive' edition of Haydn's complete works. Projected to commence with the piano music, it was advertised as being prepared with the composer's full consent and consultation. The go-between Griesinger had evidently succeeded in his task. Haydn enlisted the assistance of his old Viennese publisher Artaria in collecting subscriptions for his own printed edition of *The Creation*, and also wrote numerous letters to canvass for subscriptions from England. In particular, Charles Burney responded with typical generosity in offering to gather subscribers, and also offered the sound advice that Haydn should delay the publication of the score until after Christmas in order to catch all the potential subscribers in London (the English gentry commonly spent late sumnmer and the whole of autumn at their country estates).

At about this time Artaria published the Op. 76 string quartets, and by mid-July 1799 Haydn was at Eisenstadt, where summer was cold and rainy. The fourth of his six late masses ('Theresienmesse', Hob.XXII:12) was probably first performed at Eisenstadt on Sunday 8 September. Six days later he was back in Vienna, where his wife Maria Anna had recently made her last will and testament. Although the Haydns were ill-matched and had a long, unhappy marriage, several visitors to their house at Gumpendorf clearly state that husband and wife were co-habitating in the late 1790s, and Maria Anna made her husband her residuary legatee.

In October Haydn was back at Eisenstadt, where his relationship with Prince Nicolaus II had now thawed after its icy beginnings. The recent triumph of *The Creation* in Vienna could not have escaped Nicolaus II's attention, and he realised that Haydn was no mere servant but arguably the world's greatest living composer. For his part, Haydn must have remained grateful for the security which the Esterházy family had given him over nearly four decades: the death of his old friend Dittersdorf on 24 October 1799 in straitened circumstances must have provided a sober reminder of how celebrated composers could fall from fashion and die in poverty.

The plight of musicians was of great concern to Haydn, who decided that the next public performances of *The Creation* should be given by the Tonkünstler-Societät in aid of its fund for musicians' widows and orphans (22–23 December 1799). The charity itself was struggling, and his gift of *The Creation* ensured a popular commercial success. The decision to double ticket prices enabled the charity to survive and continue its benevolent work. Even with his self-confessed weariness, Haydn had a phenomenal work ethic: it was during 1799 that he composed his Op. 77 string quartets for Prince Lobkowitz, and supplied the first batch of his many Scottish song arrangements to the Edinburgh publisher George Thomson (he continued to send such arrangements to Thomson for the next five years).

Die Jahreszeiten ('The Seasons')

Haydn continued composing *Die Jahreszeiten* ('The Seasons') during the winter of 1799–1800. Swieten repeated the formula of beginning with an existing English text by selecting, abridging, adapting and translating an epic pastoral poem by the Scottish poet James Thomson (believed by some to have written the text for Arne's 'Rule, Britannia'). Thomson's lengthy work amounted to 5,541 lines of blank verse which had been published in five installments (one per season, and a concluding 'Hymn') from 1726 to 1730. Swieten also knew and used a German translation by the Hamburg poet Barthold

Heinrich Brockes that had been published in 1745 (Brockes had been a friend of Handel, who set several of his texts to music, including the so-called *Brockes Passion* and the nine German arias). Griesinger reported that by 5 February 1800 Haydn's work was quite far advanced, and the composer was doubtless again given encouragement and support from the Gesellschaft der Associierten, but he had some misgivings about the project. Although the text is full of descriptions of the countryside and the changing weather associated with each season, it is possible that Haydn felt the lack of a coherent narrative linking the four parts into a satisfying whole. Nor was he fully satisfied with three peasant characters – Hanne, Lucas and Simon – who are little more than generic stereotypes. Haydn famously complained that 'in *The Creation* angels speak and tell of God, but in *The Seasons* it is only Simon speaking'.

The printed score of *The Creation* eventually materialised on the last day of February 1800. Published under Haydn's own auspices but sold from Artaria's shop on the Kohlmarkt, the score featured a formidable list of 400 subscribers from all over Europe, ranging from important aristocrats (Emperor Franz II, members of the Esterházy family, Prince Schwarzenberg, George III, the Prince of Wales, the Duke of York) to loyal friends and musical colleagues (Baron van Swieten, Johann Peter Salomon, the Handel editor Dr Samuel Arnold, Dr Charles Burney, Rebecca Schroeter). *The Creation* was promptly sent all over Europe. Now that the score was accessible to the public, Artaria wasted little time in capitalising upon the oratorio's popularity. Different Viennese musicians had been commissioned to make an arrangement for string quintet and a piano vocal score respectively, and these were published only nine days after Haydn's full score.

After conducting a performance of *The Creation* in Ofen (part of modern-day Budapest) for the birthday of the Archduke Palatine, Haydn travelled to Baden to be at his wife Maria Anna's side as she lay dying. Frau Haydn passed away on 20 March 1800, at the age of seventy, and was buried two days later. It has been suggested that the elderly Haydn was relieved to be free at long last from his miserable forty-year marriage, but one suspects that in his own way he was saddened by the loss. Had Maria Anna died even a decade earlier he would have been young enough to pursue a second marriage, with Luigia Polzelli or Rebecca Schroeter. Those prospects had now faded.

On 28 March Anton Weidinger gave the public premiere of the concerto Haydn had composed four years earlier for his keyed trumpet. Incredibly, the fickle Viennese who were crazy with admiration for *The Creation* were utterly uninterested in attending this less glamorous premiere. But perhaps attention was shifting onto the unruly and revolutionary modernist Beethoven, who had grown increasingly apart from his former teacher both artistically and ideologically. The precocious rebel's Symphony No. 1 in C was dedicated to Gottfried van Swieten, and premiered at the Burgtheater on 2 April 1800. Acclaimed by the *Allgemeine musikalische Zeitung* as the most interesting concert to have occurred in Vienna for a long time, it was followed on 7 and 8 April by performances of *The Creation* by the Tonkünstler-Societät with an orchestra of 200 musicians under Haydn's direction. Despite the ticket price being restored to a normal rate (in 1799 it had been doubled), it was not the sell-out success the charity had expected. Viennese audiences, as always, were inclined to blow hot and cold, and perhaps some of fashionable society began to regard *The Creation* as 'old' music.

Meanwhile, a controversy raged in London over the performing rights to *The Creation*. Salomon, who had presented Haydn with the source libretto, was justifiably aggrieved when the first English performance of the oratorio was given at Covent Garden on 28 March 1800 by his competitor John Ashley, in a rapidly cobbled-together version using parts extracted from the printed score. Salomon advertised that his performance at the King's Theatre on 21 April had been prepared in full consultation with Haydn regarding 'the Style and Manner in which it must be executed, in order to produce the Effects required by the Author'.

Back in Vienna, Haydn had been working too hard. His health suffered from conducting concerts, composing *The Seasons*, and producing his own edition of *The Creation*. Two performances of *The Creation* at the Palais Schwarzenberg (12 and 13 April) had to be conducted by Haydn's godson Weigl because the composer fell seriously ill with rheumatic fever. He was still convalescing when he received another letter from his former mistress Luigia Polzelli demanding money, and reminding him that he was now free to marry her. He replied on 23 May 1800 with a formal statement that if he 'should consider marrying again' he would not take any wife other than Luigia. Having not seen her for a decade and presumably tired of her nagging for money, he shrewdly added that should he remain a widower he would remember Luigia in his will. Satisfied with this one-sided promise, Luigia promptly married somebody else.

Haydn's friends were alarmed that he might not recover from his illness, but in mid-June he sent another thirty-two Scottish song arrangements to George Thomson (although from this time onwards he often delegated these arrangements to his former pupil Sigismund Neukomm). In July 1800 Haydn negotiated the publication of his oratorio *The Seven Last Words* with Breitkopf & Härtel, and opened discussion with the Leipzig firm about *The Seasons*. He evidently wished to avoid the personal pressure and financial risk that his own publication of *The Creation* had caused. Still unwell, he went to Eisenstadt for the summer, where during August he wrote to Luigia Polzelli expressing hope that it would not be long before he was cured completely.

Soon Haydn received news that the British war hero Admiral Horatio Nelson and his mistress Lady Hamilton were to visit Nicolaus II at Eisenstadt on 6 September, en route from Naples to England. Reputedly a talented amateur soprano, Emma Hamilton had recently been given a score of *The Creation*, and expressed a desire to sing Haydn's cantata *Arianna a Naxos*. The composer did not have a copy with him in Eisenstadt, so he hastily asked Artaria to send him the music. Nelson and Hamilton, and a retinue of friends, family and colleagues, stayed at Eisenstadt for four days. Prince Nicolaus laid on elaborate festivities both for his visitors and for the nameday celebrations of his wife, with concerts every day, fireworks, balls and banquets. Haydn composed the song *The Battle of the Nile* (Hob.XXVIb:4) for Lady Hamilton, and later reported that she barely left his side for two days. Nelson gave Haydn a pocket-watch, and in return requested the composer's worn-out pen with which he wrote his music. The 'Nelson Mass' (*Missa in angustiis*) may have been revived during the festivities, though there is no firm evidence for this. Sidetracked by illness and committed to work on *The Seasons*, Haydn was unable to compose a new mass in 1800, but he probably unveiled his splendid new *Te Deum* (Hob.XXIIIc:2) either on 8 September, while the eminent English guests were still at Eisenstadt, or six days later at Marie Hermenegild Esterházy's nameday service. This had been commissioned by Empress Marie Therese, and it is possible that she and Emperor Franz II were present at its first performance.

Soon afterwards Haydn visited Eszterháza for the last time. The elaborate palace and estate that Nicolaus I had intended as the 'Hungarian Versailles' had been largely abandoned for a decade, and was now used only as a glorified hunting lodge; it was primarily for that purpose that the Archduke Palatine Joseph visited it in early November 1800. Haydn led a concert with a small contingent of musicians that must have seemed a far cry from the golden age of the late Nicolaus I's grand musical establishment. Haydn had never expressed much enthusiasm for life in the Hungarian wilderness, and had often succumbed to colds whilst resident in the damp reclaimed marshlands. Upon Haydn's return to Vienna, Griesinger reported to Breitkopf & Härtel that the sharp air had 'caused him disturbances'. Instead of following his usual habit of renting an apartment in the centre of Vienna during the winter, Haydn chose to remain at his house in Gumpendorf. Advancing years doubtless played a part in this decision; perhaps, too, the Gumpendorf house was more agreeable without the presence of his wife. But his health remained a serious concern. Having supervised musical performances at Eisenstadt during a visit from a large contingent of the imperial family in early December, he was too tired to direct the Tonkünstler-Societät's performances of *The Creation* just before Christmas. He was also no doubt concerned to hear that his brother Michael had been robbed at gunpoint by French soldiers during the invasion of Salzburg. Joseph promptly sent

Michael a gold watch, gold snuff-box (possibly that which he had just received from the Emperor at Eisenstadt a few weeks before), and the promise of more financial assistance.

By early 1801 a temporary peace had been struck between Austria and France, and on 16 January Haydn gave a benefit performance of *The Creation* which raised over 7,000 gulden for wounded soliders. He was reported to have conducted with 'youthful fire', and two weeks later directed two of his symphonies in a charity concert in which Beethoven also participated; but by 21 February he was confined to his bed with a fever, caught from 'too much exertion'. It took him about a month to recover, which probably further delayed completion of *The Seasons*. His job was not made any easier by his demanding and often difficult librettist Swieten, who unreasonably sought to persuade the old composer to design the music in such a way that English and French texts could be fitted to it. Swieten evidently wanted *The Seasons* to be disseminated and performed around Europe more promptly than *The Creation* had been.

The score was finished by 28 March, but it was feared that Haydn's deteriorating health would cause the oratorio's premiere to be postponed until 1802. However, the following day Haydn conducted *The Seven Last Words* for the Tonkünstler-Societät, and the Gesellschaft der Associierten set plans in motion for *The Seasons* to receive its private premiere at Prince Schwarzenberg's palace. Owing to a death in the Prince's family, the performance was postponed until 24 April 1801. The performing forces included the same three soloists who had given the first perfomance of *The Creation* three years earlier, instrumentalists from Vienna's opera orchestras (several of whom had been members of Haydn's orchestra at Eszterháza), and a chorus constituted from various church choirs. The Gesellschaft's fifteen members each paid 195 gulden to cover all performance costs, and Prince Schwarzenberg once again employed mounted police to control the public's excitement. Only rehearsals had been open to the Viennese, but the city did not have long to wait until the first public performance of *The Seasons*, which took place at the Redoutensaal on 29 May 1801. Although the Redoutensaal performance was not particularly well attended, the new oratorio was favourably received. One Viennese correspondent enthusiastically noted that Haydn had exceeded all expectation: 'The power of expression with which the artist very vividly describes nature in all its guises surpasses any description.' Another newspaper report claimed that *The Seasons* moved 'the coldest heart to the most gentle emotions'. Griesinger published a review in the *Allgemeine musikalische Zeitung*:

> *Every word, under the hands of this musical Prometheus, is full of life and perception. Sometimes the melody of the voice delights, sometimes we are shaken, as a woodland torrent that bursts over its banks, by the mighty entrance of the orchestra; now one delights in a simple, artless expression; or one admires the sumptuous richness of swift and bright harmonies. From the beginning to the end the spirit is involuntarily swept along by emotions that range from the most touching to the most terrible, from the most naïve to the most artful, from the commonplace to the most sublime.*

Although Griesinger acclaimed every line in the music as bearing 'the stamp of genius', he privately expressed less admiration for Swieten's libretto: 'Haydn has learnt the secret of the ancients, who knew how to make gold out of dross'. In fact, a few months later Haydn was surprisingly undiplomatic in his criticism of Swieten's croaking frogs as 'Frenchified trash', and declared that this 'wretched idea' had been forced upon him. Haydn also told Griesinger that he had found the concept of a hymn to hard toil absurdly unrealistic, and there is plenty of anecdotal evidence that Haydn frequently rowed with Swieten over the latter's pompous suggestions. However, the oratorio was sufficiently popular for Breitkopf & Härtel to pay 4,500 gulden, thereby beating stiff competition from several companies for exclusive publication rights.

Last years

On 5 May 1801 Haydn made his first will, partly out of a desire to ensure that his family and close associates would be sufficiently provided for. His two brothers were the beneficiaries of the most substantial bequests, and the enigmatic bequest of a considerable sum (1,000 gulden) to Princess Graschalkowitz's maidservant Catherine Csech suggests that perhaps he had enjoyed the companionship of a mistress before Luigia Polzelli (the Italian singer was bequeathed an annual pension of 150 gulden). For the remainder of his life Haydn frequently made small changes to his will, but in the wake of *The Seasons* he had become increasingly conscious of his own mortality.

In the meantime, he had received the special gift of a new grand piano from Érard in Paris. On 20 May he appreciatively wrote to Érard that the piano was 'the greatest masterpiece of its kind I have ever seen or heard'. By July 1801 Haydn was attending to his duties in Eisenstadt, where

Prince Nicolaus II had re-engaged the Feldharmonie eight months earlier. This must have come as an enormous relief to its members, who in the last three years had struggled to eke out an adequate living. Some (if not all) of the Feldharmonie players took part in the first performance of their Kapellmeister's new mass on 13 September in Eisenstadt's Bergkirche (Hob.XXII:13, nicknamed the 'Schöpfungsmesse' ('Creation Mass') because of Haydn's witty use of a self-quotation from Adam and Eve's duet at 'Qui tollis peccata mundi'). The sixty-nine-year-old composer had only just completed and prepared his new masterpiece in time for Princess Marie Hermenegild's nameday service; one anecdote recounts that during the performance he 'darted like a weasel' to the organ in time to play the solo during the 'Et incarnatus est'. Maybe his visiting brother Michael was persuaded to participate as a performer. It was perhaps at around this time that Prince Nicolaus II, aware that his own Haydn could not continue forever, offered Michael the position of vice-Kapellmeister at Eisenstadt. Though tempted, Michael refused – possibly on the advice of his older brother – and decided to remain at the Salzburg court for the rest of his life.

Back in his little house at Gumpendorf by the end of October, Haydn might have heard – and been moved by – a performance of one of his masses in St Stephen's Cathedral, where he had sung as a choirboy in the 1740s, on 25 October 1801. Rumours began to circulate that the Haydn–Swieten partnership was to produce more new works, ranging from an oratorio depicting the Last Judgement to more comic subjects. Swieten seems to have initiated some of these ideas himself in order to 'convince the world of Haydn's all-embracing genius', but Haydn was neither inclined to embark on an exhausting new collaboration, nor anxious to prove anything to anyone. Military conflicts notwithstanding, the first Parisian performance of *The Creation* had provoked such an outpouring of adulation that a specially made gold medal was sent to Haydn. He had never managed to fulfil his ambition to visit Paris; after seriously pondering whether to do so now, he decided against any more long journeys. This prudence was entirely sensible. As the year drew to a close he regularly suffered from severe colds.

Despite his advancing years and frequent bouts of exhaustion and illness, Haydn did not forsake his friends and official duties. In early December 1801 he negotiated with Prince Nicolaus II for an increase in the salary of his old violinist friend Luigi Tomasini. On 22 and 23 December he conducted charity performances of *The Seasons* for the Tonkünstler-Societät at the Burgtheater (at which he received an ovation from the packed audiences), and four days later he conducted *The Creation* in aid of the poor who lived in the St Marx district of the imperial city.

At the beginning of 1802 Haydn was again afflicted by the recurring problem of a polyp in his nose, and was confined to his rooms for over a week. In the early spring he received an unexpected offer from Salieri to produce *La vera costanza* at the Court Opera. His operas, the product of a bygone age, had been performed quite frequently in German translation in provincial theatres, but had never secured a place in the most prestigious opera house in his home city. Although he realised that accepting Salieri's offer would have redressed the wrongs done in 1778 (if *La vera costanza* was indeed intended for Vienna and had its performance thwarted by cabals), Haydn refused because an agreement could not be reached about casting the principal role of Rosina. On or around 31 March 1802 Haydn celebrated his seventieth birthday without pomp, and on Palm Sunday (11 April) he conducted the Tonkünstler-Societät's performance of *The Seasons*.

Many eminent people, including Empress Marie Therese, urged him to undertake one more large-scale work, but he held back from doing so until he could find a 'useful' text. He expressed an interest in working with the famous poet Wieland, but the old German author could not be persuaded to collaborate. During June 1802 Haydn began writing a new mass for Princess Marie Hermenegild (Hob.XXII:14, nicknamed 'Harmoniemesse' because of its prominent use of the expanded Feldharmonie). On 29 July he was visited by Prince Nicolaus II, who politely requested that his Kapellmeister accompany him to Eisenstadt the following week. The sympathetic Prince continued to search for a vice-Kapellmeister, and on 14 August he notified Haydn that he had appointed the native Eisenstadt musician Johann Nepomuk Fuchs, whose duties were to assist 'the direction of the orchestra and church music in your absence'. Just as Haydn had himself been primed to succeed Gregor Werner many years before, so his successor was now in place (although in future years the Esterházys' annual celebratory masses were frequently entrusted to Hummel, and once, in 1807, to Beethoven).

Haydn's 'Harmoniemesse', his last major composition, was performed under his direction on Wednesday 8 September 1802 in the Bergkirche at Eisenstadt. An eyewitness of the Princess's nameday celebrations observed that the composer – once regarded as a senior servant rather than a social equal – dined with the illustrious princely guests whilst the musicians played 'Tafelmusik', and that one of the after-dinner toasts was given in honour to the elderly composer. Haydn's relationship with Nicolaus II had started badly, but a measure of the Prince's genuine respect and affection for his diligent Kapellmeister is also evident in the generous gift of an annual supply of expensive wine.

By the end of September Haydn had returned home to Vienna, where he wrote a warm reply to a letter he had received from a group of musicians from the German island of Rugen (in the North Sea):

It was indeed a most pleasant surprise to me to receive such a flattering letter from a place where I could have no idea that the fruits of my poor talents were known... What happiness does this thought cause me! Often, when contending with the obstacles of every sort that interfered with my work, when my powers of both body and mind were failing and I felt it a hard matter to persevere in the course I had entered on, a secret feeling whispered, 'There are but few contented and happy men here below; everywhere grief and care prevail; perhaps your labours may one day be the source from which the weary and worn, or the man burdened with affairs, may derive a few moments of rest and refreshment.' What a powerful motive for pressing onwards! And this is why I now look back with heartfelt and cheerful satisfaction on the labours expended on this art, to which I have devoted so long a succession of years and such persevering efforts and exertions.

At the end of November Haydn composed his last completed instrumental work, the Hungarian National March (Hob.VIII:4). A few days later he wrote to his former pupil and London rival Pleyel: 'I wish that I could have back 10 years of my advanced age, so that I could [compose]... perhaps – despite everything – it can still happen...'

Despite conducting charity performances of both

The Creation and *The Seasons* in December 1802, the septuagenarian's days as an active composer and Kapellmeister were now over. The possibility of collaborating with Gottfried van Swieten on an oratorio on the Last Judgement disappeared when the Baron died on 29 March 1803. Even if a suitable text had been found, it is unlikely that Haydn would have had the energy to set it to music. He had recently written to his brother Michael, complaining about a 'continual nervous weakness' that had plagued him for five months.

Rather than continue his accustomed habit of trading and negotiating with numerous publishers across Europe, Haydn now preferred to place his trust in Breitkopf & Härtel's endeavour to publish his complete works in installments. It is touchingly sad to read his letter to the Leipzig firm in which he commented:

> It is almost as if with the decline in my mental powers, my desire and compulsion to work increase. O God! how much remains to be done in this glorious art, even by such a man as I have been!

On 10 May 1803 the Vienna city authorities awarded Haydn a 'twelve-fold golden citizen's medal' in gratitude for his benevolent support of the city's charities. He responded with customary charm and courtesy: 'I shall prize it... during all the remaining days that Providence sees fit to allow me.' Yet at about this time he realised that he was incapable of finishing several compositions that he had attempted to start, and a secretary from the British embassy noted that Haydn 'desired nothing so much as to pass the short time he has yet to live in repose and quiet.' He spent the summer of 1803 in Eisenstadt; it is unlikely that he was expected to do any conducting, but he still had some administrative duties and may have revised his old *Stabat mater* for Princess Esterházy's nameday service. He conducted a charity concert, including *The Seven Last Words*, on 26 December 1803; this was his last public performance.

Retired from public life, Haydn seldom left his house. Early in 1804 Griesinger visited, and found him bitterly lamenting the wet weather, and confiding that he could not work for more than half an hour without becoming dizzy. Haydn also candidly commented on the arrogance of Beethoven (the schism in the relationship between the two composers seems to have been largely caused by the petulance, jealousy and ingratitude of the younger man). On 1 April the Viennese government granted Haydn the freedom of the city. Neither was the retired seventy-two-year-old forgotten by his friends in London. On 12 April he received a letter from Salomon which included the proceeds from the score of *The Creation*, collected by Burney.

At about this time Haydn presumably resigned all his responsibilities at the Esterházy court to vice-Kapellmeister Fuchs and the recently appointed concertmaster Johann Nepomuk Hummel, a pupil of Mozart who became a highly successful and respected composer in his own right. For the first time in years, Haydn was not required to travel to Eisenstadt, and on 28 September 1804 he declined Hummel's invitation to conduct *The Creation* there. On 10 November the *Wiener Zeitung* announced the publication of six fugues arranged by Haydn from oratorios that had been composed by his Esterházy predecessor Gregor Werner. Perhaps this peculiarly antiquarian project was a private personal gesture as Haydn's own life drew towards a close. However, he was amused to discover that premature reports of his death had inspired Cherubini to compose a funeral cantata and organise its performance in Paris. Apparently Haydn remarked, 'If I had known about the ceremony I would have gone there myself to conduct the Requiem in person!'

He was too weak to attend a concert organised to celebrate his seventy-third birthday, at which Franz Xaver Mozart made his public debut; but he still had sufficient energy to make an attempt to put his personal music library in order. With help from his long-serving copyist Elssler, Haydn used the opportunity to make a complete catalogue of his own works. This was eventually titled the 'Catalogue of all those compositions that I approximately recall having composed from my 18th to my 73rd year'. It was completed in August 1805, and a copy was sent to Breitkopf & Härtel.

Haydn continued to receive visitors, including his biographers Griesinger (who found him to grow 'more fragile') and Albert Christoph Dies, Cherubini (perhaps checking that Haydn was in sufficiently good health for his funeral cantata to remain on ice), the London-based keyboard virtuoso and publisher Muzio Clementi, and the aspiring young composer Carl Maria von Weber. Pleyel found Haydn 'continually praying with a rosary', and remarked that he 'looks as if he were more than eighty'. In fact, Haydn was now in the first stages of protracted terminal arteriosclerosis. Princess Marie Hermenegild Esterházy visited Gumpendorf several times, including an occasion on which she had to break the news that Haydn's youngest brother Johann had died on 10 May 1805 in Eisenstadt.

In the meantime the Napoleonic Wars had exploded across Europe again. The imperial court had fled Vienna shortly before the French assumed control of the city on 13 November 1805. Napoleon set up quarters at Schönbrunn and attended concerts, but showed no apparent interest in the elderly Haydn. A peace treaty was signed on 26 December, the French left Vienna, and things temporarily returned to normal (albeit with tremendous inflation and political instability); but Haydn's sadness at the changing world must have deepened further when he belatedly received news that his other brother Michael had died in Salzburg on 10 August 1806. In contrast, he was given cause for joy when his fears about financial problems were allayed by the Esterházys' sensitive gift of an extra 600 gulden per annum. The Prince wrote that his wife had suggested the idea in order to give Haydn 'a great source of comfort and consolation', and remarked: 'It is with great pleasure that I hasten to use this opportunity to show my esteem and friendship for you'.

Haydn was no longer able to write his own letters, but dictated a heartfelt response thanking Prince Nicolaus II for 'this undeserved act of special grace': 'I am unable to describe my most heartfelt thanks for this most gracious of acts, extended to an old and feeble servant.'

The Prince's affection for his retired Kapellmeister was also evident in his commission of a portrait by Isidor Neugass. Completed in December 1806, it shows the composer holding pages of *The Creation* in his hand. A couple of months later he recovered from another illness and joked to Dies that he had escaped death once again, but Empress Marie Therese was not as fortunate: she and her new-born baby died in April 1807. By this time Haydn's doctors had removed the little piano from his bedroom to spare his frustrated efforts to play and compose. On 3 September 1807 he told Griesinger: 'I would never have believed that a man could fall to pieces as thoroughly... My memory is gone. Sometimes I still have good ideas at the piano, but I feel like weeping at my inability to repeat them and write them down.'

A visitor to Gumpendorf in November 1807 remarked that Haydn still had fire in his eyes and a 'charming joviality'. On New Year's Eve he had a special visit from Mozart's widow Constanze, during which he wept at the mention of her late husband's name. It seems that Antonio Polzelli (whom his mother Luigia alleged to be Haydn's son) and members of the Esterházy orchestra sent a touching letter of congratulation to Haydn on his nameday in March 1808. To celebrate the composer's forthcoming seventy-sixth birthday, Prince Trauttmannsdorf sponsored a gala performance of *The Creation* on 27 March 1808 in the great hall of the university, sung in Italian under the direction of Salieri. Haydn was determined to attend, telling Griesinger that he wanted to show that he was still capable of graciously receiving the honour. Prince Nicolaus II arranged for one of his carriages to drive Haydn slowly into the city centre, where the large crowd had to be controlled by police. Greeted on his arrival by a party including Prince Lobkowitz, Princess Esterházy, Hummel, Salieri and Beethoven, Haydn was placed in an armchair and carried into the hall, accompanied by trumpet and timpani fanfares, and an applauding public who cried out 'Long live Haydn!' The old composer felt cold, at which Princess Esterházy and other aristocratic ladies placed their own shawls over his legs. The occasion must have been deeply moving for Haydn, who was presented with poems in his honour and publicly embraced by Salieri. During the first part of *The Creation* tears ran down his cheeks. The frail old man could not cope, and left after 'Die Himmel erzählen die Ehre

Gottes' ('The Heavens are telling the glory of God') to the sound of a tremendous ovation. This was to be Haydn's last public appearance.

Housebound and cared for by his faithful assistant Elssler and several servants, Haydn was prone to nostalgia. He played 'Gott erhalte Franz den Kaiser' at his piano several times every day. Prince Esterházy took upon himself all his retired Kapellmeister's increasingly expensive medical costs, and on 7 February 1809 Haydn made his final will. His estate amounted to about 55,000 gulden, but the deaths of both his younger brothers necessitated alterations. Shortly after his seventy-seventh birthday, Austria foolishly declared war on France once more. By 9 April 1809 the Viennese were preparing to defend the city against Napoleon again. Haydn was distraught about the resurgence of the Napoleonic Wars, and his poor health rapidly declined. His little house at Gumpendorf, often described by visitors as a peaceful retreat, was caught in the crossfire between the Viennese and French artillery during the bombardment of Vienna on 11–12 May (his nerves were badly affected when a cannonball fell in his courtyard and blew his bedroom door open). On 13 May Vienna surrendered. Napoleon, aware that the great Haydn was frail, ordered that a guard of honour be stationed at his house.

On 24 May 1809 Haydn received his last visitor. A French officer from the Hussars paid his respects to the composer, and the two men enjoyed an animated conversation about *The Creation*. The French officer sang the tenor aria 'Mit Würd' und Hoheit angetan' ('In native worth'), in Italian, with such tenderness that Haydn exclaimed that he could not recall any song having given him so much real pleasure. The French officer rode off to rejoin his regiment.

Haydn's house in Vienna

His exact identity is unknown, but it is unlikely that he survived the war.

Elssler described that Haydn played the 'Emperor's Hymn' for the last time on 26 May, 'with such expression and taste... that our good Papa was astonished about it himself'. Feeling unwell, Haydn had to be helped into bed at five o'clock in the afternoon, shivering and complaining of a headache. Despite sleeping better than usual that night, he was too weak to rise from his bed the following morning. Elssler wrote to Griesinger that:

> *The numbing got much worse, but so quietly and willing in everything that we were all astonished, our good Papa didn't complain of any pains... despite all kinds of medicines administered... Papa got steadily weaker and quieter...*

149

On 31 May 1809, at about twenty minutes before one o'clock in the morning, Haydn passed away 'quietly and peacefully'. Owing to the war it was only possible to arrange a simple burial in the local cemetery at Gumpendorf, which took place at five o'clock the next afternoon (his remains are now interred in a mausoleum in Eisenstadt's Bergkirche that Prince Nicolaus Esterházy II constructed in 1820). One of the few who attended remarked that 'Not one Viennese Kapellmeister was in the funeral cortège', but these were far from ordinary times. A requiem by Michael Haydn was performed in Gumpendorf under difficult circumstances, but a more suitable public tribute was organised on 15 June. This was in Vienna's Schottenkirche and included a solemn mass as well as a performance of Mozart's Requiem by the Tonkünstler-Societät. French officials and army officers attended together with the Viennese aristocratic élite. It was a remarkable and entirely fitting indication of the esteem in which Papa Haydn was held across Europe.

Haydn's music transcended political concerns, language barriers and cultural differences, as it continues to do today. He was one of the first great composers to achieve fame in his own lifetime that endured after his death. Although tastes changed during the nineteenth century (and shall always continue to transform with the passage of time), and aspects of his music diminished in the eyes of critics, writers and musicians, Haydn's reputation has remained generally respected – even if at times his music has been misunderstood or underrated by those preferring to concentrate on Mozart's dramatic insight and Beethoven's revolutionary fervour. The last half of the twentieth century witnessed an enormous surge in the attention devoted to Haydn's church music, operas and less popular symphonies. At the time of writing, Haydn's music is probably more widely disseminated (mainly through recordings), and his achievements more generously respected and admired, than at any time since his death. Some of his lesser works, including many of the baryton trios, are still rarely performed, and have yet to be recorded. But it has become easy to discern the wisdom in Haydn's remark to Mozart in 1790: 'My language is understood all over the whole world!'

Symphonies

Haydn did not invent the Classical symphony, but his contribution to the genre was fundamental to its development into a sophisticated art form. It is generally accepted that Haydn composed 106 symphonies, although many more were attributed to him during the eighteenth century. He considered that the Symphony No. 1 in D, composed for Count Morzin in about 1757, was his first proper symphony, and his first symphonic masterpieces for the Esterházy family were Nos 6–8 ('Le Matin', 'Le Midi' and 'Le Soir'), written in 1761. During the late 1760s and early 1770s, Haydn became increasingly fond of writing symphonies in a style that later came to be identified with the literary movement *Sturm und Drang* ('Storm and Stress'), in which tempestuous fast movements, bustling string textures, and sudden dramatic changes in dynamic created considerable tension. However, so-called *Sturm und Drang* symphonies such as No. 26 ('Lamentation'), No. 45 ('Farewell') and No. 49 ('La passione') also contained movements of tender elegance that do not conform to the label. By the end of the decade Haydn had largely moved away from *Sturm und Drang*, and instead concentrated on achieving a sense of flamboyance and playfulness in his symphonies. Like any popular composer of the age, he had developed the ability to write crowd-pleasing works in which learned technical mastery was subtly embedded in the music without preventing its accessibility to a casual audience at first hearing.

His symphonies composed during the early 1780s are a clever synthesis between an appealing galant style and the more profound dramatic nature of the seemingly unbridled passions evident in the *Sturm und Drang* works. However, the invitation received in 1784/5 to compose six works especially for Paris enabled Haydn to broaden his symphonic horizons. It seems that the orchestra of the concert organisation Concert de la Loge Olympique only permitted freemasons to play in it; they wore elaborate uniforms of sky-blue dress coats with lace ruffles, and, unlike the humble musicians at Eszterháza, the well-to-do Parisian players wore their swords during concerts. The French musicians were clearly not foppish slouches, though, and the music Haydn composed for them suggests that they had an excellent command of musical matters. He explored the range of formal and expressive possibilities offered by a set of six symphonies. With notably varied forms of slow movements (*Allegretto* double variations in No. 82, an expansive sonata-form *Andante* for No. 83, *Andante* variations in 6/8 time in No. 84, variations on the French song *La gentille et jeune Lisette* in No. 85, a *Largo* for No. 86 headed *Capriccio*, and a beautiful *Adagio* for No. 87 with prominent parts for woodwind), grandly dramatic fast movements, and an uncanny genius for combining brilliance, wit, inventiveness, elegance, and subtly detailed form, Haydn challenged the listener in a manner that had scarcely before been achieved in orchestral music. Perhaps he was aware of the musical impact that could be made by the huge forces of the Concert de la Loge Olympique, but, if so, he was also canny enough to write most of the six symphonies (the exceptions are Nos 82 and 86, both with trumpets and drums) for a basic instrumentation of flute, oboes, bassoons, horns and strings, with an eye to performance by more modestly scaled groups outside Paris.

Haydn's last twelve symphonies for London were written in three clusters: Nos 93–98 for Salomon's concerts at the Hanover Square Rooms in 1791–2, Nos 99–101 for Salomon's 1794 concert season, and Nos 102–4 for the joint venture at the King's Theatre concert room in 1795. Haydn's vivacious music in these twelve symphonies reached a new artistic peak: appealing tunefulness was perfectly allied with sustained dramatic moods, grand effects and colourful orchestration. Flutes, clarinets (used in Nos 99–101, 103 and 104), trumpets and drums were expected in London orchestras during the early 1790s, and Haydn relished the opportunity to exploit the textural possibilities offered by new instrumental combinations. The results must have seemed like a dazzling myriad of unusual sounds to an eighteenth-century audience.

Some of the symphonies were unorthodox and featured blatant novelties (e.g. No. 94 'The Surprise'), whereas others were more subtly original. The composer meticulously crafted a succession of symphonies that demonstrated his versatility and expressive range, and he also seems to have ensured that each work possessed a prominent individual tag that could identify it. For example, the humorous use of a flatulent bassoon in the *Largo cantabile* of No. 93, the lyrical solo cello in the Minuet of No. 95, the passage marked 'sul ponticello' (instructing the string players to bow near the bridge of their instruments) in the *Adagio* of No. 97, the short fortepiano solo in the coda of the finale to No. 98, the beautiful woodwind passage in the *Adagio* of No. 99, the Turkish-style 'military' percussion in the *Allegretto* of No. 100, the tick-tock 'clock' beat in the *Andante* of No. 101, and the drumroll in No. 103. Typically for Haydn, his compositions presented an unparalleled union of experimentation and broad appeal to a general audience.

Concertos

Haydn wrote numerous concertos, especially in the 1760s, but the genre was never a central part of his activities. The solo parts in his earliest keyboard concertos were probably played by the composer on the organ, but otherwise he did not perform as a concerto soloist (unlike Mozart and Beethoven, both renowned for starring as the soloists in their own concertos, designed to demonstrate their own prowess). The concerto was less popular in mid-eighteenth century Vienna than the symphony, and was perhaps the least progressive genre in which Haydn worked. His earliest concertos generally follow the same plan of fast–slow–fast movements that had been developed by Vivaldi and Tartini in Italy, decades earlier, with four tutti ritornellos from the orchestra interspersed with three sections showcasing the virtuosity and expressive capabilities of the solo instrument. Moreover, Haydn's concertos are usually much shorter than the adventurous extended concertos written for Vienna by Mozart two decades later, or by Beethoven at the turn of the century.

However, the development of sonata-form movements in concertos expanded the possibilities of the solo instrument's contribution, and the inventive way in which Haydn wrote for soloists from the Esterházy Capelle resulted in some magnificent and enjoyable works (such as the Cello Concerto in C, Hob.VIIb:1, widely acknowledged as one of the finest concertos of the age). In later years Haydn seldom composed concertos because there was no practical purpose in doing so. One exception is the Trumpet Concerto in E flat (Hob.VIIe:1) of 1796. Compared with the elegant but conventionally conceived earlier concertos, the Trumpet Concerto was written for a larger orchestra, and featured increased interaction between soloist and accompaniment. It was Haydn's last major orchestral work, and it is his masterpiece in the concerto genre.

Keyboard Music

Early Keyboard Works

Most of Haydn's solo keyboard works contain between two and four movements. He described most of these as 'divertimento' or 'partita' until 1771, when he employed the term 'sonata' for the first time. Haydn's thematic material is not always as distinguished and strongly characterised as the themes in keyboard works by Mozart and Beethoven, although it seems certain that much of his surviving early keyboard music was written to aid his teaching of pupils. It seems that Haydn's great strength as a keyboard composer (and, presumably, as a player too) was in his imaginative ability to vary and develop material, and in his characteristic wit. Such elements are evident from the outset of his career as an active composer: they are present in his early sets of keyboard variations, and also in trios (in which the keyboard was accompanied by two other instruments, usually violin and cello; they would either revel in canonic imitation or the keyboard would dominate proceedings, with supporting harmony notes from the other instruments). In the later 1760s, Haydn developed a more elaborate character in his keyboard writing, showing greater freedom and exploiting a wider range of dynamics, tonalities, and sonorities. By this time, he had discovered and become profoundly influenced by keyboard sonatas of Carl Philipp Emanuel Bach, probably the 'Prussian' sonatas, published in 1742 and dedicated to Bach's employer Frederick the Great. Haydn reminisced:

> When I was sitting at my old, worm-eaten clavichord, even as the snow settled on my bedclothes, I envied no king his wealth or happiness... It was during this period, too, that I came upon the first six sonatas of Emanuel Bach. I didn't leave my clavier until I had mastered them all, after which I played them many times for my own delight, especially when I felt oppressed or discouraged.

He would later study C.P.E. Bach's theoretical writings when they became available in Vienna, and acknowledged that:

Anyone who knows my music well can hear what a big debt I owe to this great man, and will see how well I understood him, having studied his music with the most unceasing industry and care.

Mature Piano Works

During the 1770s the harpsichord was progressively replaced by the fortepiano, and during this decade Haydn became a productive composer of sonatas. Although the music of seven 'expressive' sonatas (c. 1765–1771) is complex and emotionally telling, perhaps owing to the influence of C.P.E. Bach, it is notable that many of the mature Haydn's subsequent piano sonatas and solo works deliberately avoided rhetorical complexity and ornate extravagance. Instead, the composer pursued a *galant* style in three-movement sonatas that would have commercial appeal for aristocratic ladies as well as professional musicians. It is unlikely that he wrote much of this repertoire specifically for his own use; he certainly viewed his piano sonatas as commodities to sell to the highest bidder, and from 1780 onwards he peddled such works between publishers all over Europe. His production of piano music declined during the last two decades of his compositional career, but his work continued to explore the sonorities of the instrument, and grew increasingly sophisticated and penetrating in its treatment of thematic material.

String Quartets

Before the eighteenth century there was already a long tradition of performing instrumental works with one instrument per part, often with four stringed instruments echoing the layout and interaction of SATB singers in polyphonic church music (for example, English viol music from Tudor times through to Purcell). During the mid-eighteenth century, instrumental chamber music was commonly used either for indoor entertainment during meals (such as 'Tafelmusik') or outdoor serenades. However, Haydn played the decisive role in the development of the string quartet genre as sophisticated musical discourse principally designed for and appreciated by connoisseurs. By the end of the century it was widely considered the superior form of chamber music, although it remained an essentially private form of music-making: there are no reports of any public performances of string quartets in Vienna during Haydn's lifetime. Goethe once said that 'a good quartet is like listening to a stimulating conversation between four intelligent people', and this quality of democratic clarity between all four parts became increasingly abundant in Haydn's sixty-eight original quartets. These were normally published in sets of three or six, although, confusingly, opus numbers varied between different publishers across Europe.

Like Haydn's church music, his string quartets span his entire working life. His first essays in the genre during the late 1750s (Op. 1 and Op. 2) were both polished, lightweight collections written for outdoor summer parties given by his patron Baron Fürnberg, and it can be argued that the musical style descended from the Baroque tradition of chamber concertos (which would originally have featured keyboard continuo, and dense contrapuntal four-part string writing). During the 1760s Haydn's chamber music activities revolved around Prince Nicolaus's insatiable appetite for baryton music. When the composer eventually returned to the string quartet in about 1769, he did so with renewed vigour and inventiveness. It seems likely that his experience of writing in a relatively confined way for the Prince's baryton trios had whetted his appetite for exploring the potential of a group in which two violins, viola and cello all interract as soloists within a coherent whole. Op. 9

(c. 1769), with thoughtfully spaced writing for all four instruments, a greater tone of seriousness, several sombre, minor-keyed movements full of harmonic daring, and a newly established four-movement structure for each quartet, was a massive leap forward from the serenade-like early quartets. Op. 17, the earliest quartets to survive in the composer's autograph (1771), continued apace with the development of the genre as an exquisite form of subtle expression that demanded the listener's close attention, especially in their entertaining and spirited final movements. Op. 20 (1772), often regarded as Haydn's first mature quartets, introduced a more learned idiom into the quartet genre, above all in the fugal finales of Nos 2, 5 and 6.

After another break of almost a decade, during which Haydn was preoccupied with operatic duties at Eszterháza, he composed his next set of quartets in 1781 (Op. 33, which he described as being 'written in a new and special way'). Thereafter, the composer's involvement with the genre was more regular. He composed four sets between 1787 and 1790 (Opp. 50, 54, 55 and 64) that consistently marry accessibility (including evocations of vigorous folk dances) and technical sophistication. Musical rhetoric is manipulated to novel, often humorous, ends. Haydn is always likely to surprise his listeners with sudden key changes, bizarre silences or unexpected turns of phrase. The quartets of Op. 71 and Op. 74 (three in each set) were written in Vienna in 1793 for public performances during Haydn's second London visit; the Op. 76 quartets (composed in 1796–7, published in 1799) were described by Charles Burney as 'full of invention, fire, good taste, and new effects'. His last set, Op. 77, contained only two quartets (composed in 1799 and published in 1802), because the elderly composer was drained by the effort he devoted to his oratorio *The Seasons*. Yet, as the Haydn scholar David Wyn Jones has noted, the music shows 'no sign of weariness'. Although the composer's modern reputation as the 'father of the symphony' may be reasonably questioned, there is no doubt that he was the prime instigator of the string quartet as an elevated form of high musical art.

Operas

With his increasingly intensive duties at Eszterháza, Haydn was one of the most active opera composers of the late eighteenth century. Yet, for all his industry and mastery, his operas never gained repute in the leading operatic centres of the age, such as Paris, Naples, Venice, Milan, London, and even Vienna. His earliest Viennese Singspiels (German operas with spoken dialogue instead of recitatives) have not survived, and several of his early Eszterháza operas were written for the marionette theatre; there are no contemporary reports about the music, although it seems that the all-round production values were high.

Notwithstanding the fame of Gluck and Calzabigi's Italian 'reform' operas *Orfeo ed Euridice* and *Alceste*, the predominant fashion in 1760s Vienna was French opera. Prince Nicolaus's taste, on the other hand, was for Italian opera. Although Haydn never visited Italy, as a composer of vocal music he was essentially influenced by Italian styles, and it is known that he valued Galuppi, Porpora, Hasse and Gluck (even if not all were Italian-born, each composer was fundamentally Italianate in principle). In addition to selecting, arranging, rehearsing and performing operas by all the leading opera composers of the age for Prince Nicolaus's custombuilt theatre, Haydn also composed and performed a dozen of his own full-scale Italian operas between the early 1760s and 1784. These were in a broad variety of genres, from a *festa teatrale* (a short, serious entertainment for a festive celebration) such as *Acide* (premiered in January 1763), to short intermezzos such as *La canterina* (1766). However, Haydn's operatic output centred on comic *opera buffa*, which during the 1770s gradually overtook *opera seria* as the predominant genre across Europe. Haydn's priorities rested firmly on displaying the musical skills of his singers (and, of course, his own talent). Arias, usually in *da capo* or sonata form, tended to display the singer's coloratura prowess, and accompaniments were designed to illustrate the taste and ability of the orchestral musicians. Later commentators have somewhat unfairly criticised such characteristics as anti-dramatic, but these were common priorities in the eighteenth century and would not have been perceived as problems by contemporary audiences anywhere in Europe. *L'infedeltà delusa* (1773), with its long arias and ensembles, illustrates that Haydn's first priority was to give musical delight.

Haydn's Eszterháza operas seem leisurely and slow-paced from a dramatic point of view, but it is unfair to describe his mature theatrical works as 'undramatic'. They may not possess the taut psychological edge evident in Mozart's famous Da Ponte comedies of the later 1780s, but it is worth remembering that most of Haydn's operas were composed in the decade before Mozart achieved full theatrical mastery. Intense forward momentum in plot was alien to the musico-dramatic aesthetics of the 1770s and early 1780s, when enjoying the ride was more important than how fast one arrived at the final destination. Haydn's fertile musical imagination alone makes his operas well worth investigation, but his dramatic characterisations are not without interest; he often paints gently ironic portraits of his characters (such as in the fusion of comic and serious parts in the 1782 opera *Orlando paladino*, where the characters are rarely what they profess to be), and he portrays the emotional responses of characters in arias as efficiently and engagingly as any of his peers. During the 1780s Prince Nicolaus became increasingly interested in *opera seria*, even though the genre was becoming less popular in the outside world. Haydn responded to this with his ambitious serious work *Armida* (1784); it is a pity that this original and richly varied work was his last Eszterháza opera.

The principal reason why he is not a celebrated opera composer today arguably remains the same now as it did in his own lifetime: his ability to tailor a music drama for the strengths of a specific group of singers and players restricted the wider dissemination of his operas. More significantly, he simply never got the chance to prove himself at the highest level in one of Europe's leading operatic centres. To over-simplify a little, Haydn is not a famous opera composer today owing to plain bad luck; perhaps, too, because Mozart's operas from *Figaro* onwards more effectively transcend their age and the circumstances for which they were written.

Church Music

Haydn's earliest formal musical training was as a church chorister, and his first attempts at composition concentrated upon sacred music. In these respects, he shared a common heritage with almost all the composers who had preceded him in the history of the western Classical tradition, whether Catholic or Protestant. Most of the Latin texts set by Haydn were established as part of the Catholic liturgy by the Council of Trent (1545–63) during the Counter-Reformation, and his church music falls loosely into three periods. His first compositions in the genre were written between the late 1740s and mid-1750s. After a lull during his years as Kapellmeister to Count Morzin and, from 1761, Esterházy vice-Kapellmeister, Haydn composed regularly for the church between 1766, when he was appointed full Kapellmeister, and 1772. His liturgical output then tailed off when Prince Nicolaus's passion for opera came to dominate musical life at Eszterháza. His last and most glorious phase of sacred works comprised the series of six masses for Eisenstadt and a setting of the *Te Deum*, all written between 1796 and 1802.

Although Haydn's first attempts at sacred music were modestly scaled masses, his earliest sacred masterpiece was the *Salve regina* in E (Hob.XXIIIb:1), a beautiful and emotive motet written in 1756, perhaps for the service in which his love Therese Keller took the veil. It is a typically Italianate work in which a solo soprano displays expressive coloratura, and is accompanied by two violins and continuo (including organ). A small chorus contributes to simple but effective homophonic movements. Haydn composed a major sacred work almost every year in Eisenstadt between 1766 and 1772. His 1767 setting of the *Stabat mater* – a thirteen-verse medieval contemplation of the lamentation of the Virgin Mary at the Crucifixion – proved to be the most frequently performed and most widely disseminated work in his lifetime, used both liturgically and as a popular concert work. Haydn was probably familiar with powerful versions by Palestrina and Pergolesi from his childhood as a chorister in St Stephen's Cathedral. With its predominance of minor keys and slow tempos, the work avoids vocal and orchestral display in favour of mournful or elegiac expression.

Most of Haydn's fourteen masses are radiant, optimistic and

beguiling for precisely the opposite reasons: light, flowing tempos, sunny major keys, colourful orchestral effects (such as lyrical use of woodwind, dramatic brass, or colourful organ solos) combine to delight the listener, and the composer consistently shows his mastery of strict contrapuntal choral fugal writing, ritornello arias, modern symphonic orchestration and theatrical timing. Some masses for Eisenstadt, such as the 'Grosse Orgelsolomesse' (Hob.XXII:4) and the *Missa Cellensis in honorem BVM* (Hob.XXII: 5, nowadays often known under the inauthentic title 'Missa Sanctae Caeciliae'), are large-scale works with extensive passages for solo voices, grand choruses and rich orchestral accompaniment. But he could also compose concise and intimate church music for small groups of performers, such as the delicately beautiful 'Kleine Orgelsolomesse' of c. 1775–7 (Hob.XXII:7).

Haydn's six late masses feature dramatic symphonic use of orchestra (whether tender and soft with woodwind in major keys, abrasive and turbulent in minor keys, or splendidly life-affirming with brass and drums). Operatically conceived solo vocal passages lend an emotive personal element to the masses, ranging from the tender settings of the text 'Et incarnatus est' to the impassioned calls of 'Kyrie eleison' from the soprano soloist in the opening of the so-called 'Nelson Mass' (Hob.XXII:11). Although Haydn's church music is frequently thrilling or charmingly elegant, it is never insincere or superficial. Indeed, some of his late works – such as the Benedictus of the 'Nelson Mass' – contain darker, more troubled movements that bespeak uncertainty in times of political anguish (and penitential imploring, which was no less important to the devout composer and the congregation). The glorious music of the six late masses and the exciting short *Te Deum* (1799–1800) gives a strong insight into the composer's Catholic faith, which Griesinger described as 'not of the gloomy, tormented kind, but rather cheerful and reconciled'. It is perhaps regrettable that our modern-day experience of this music as seamless concert works obscures the fact that each individual movement was intended to be heard at a different position within the church service.

Oratorios

By the late 1790s, Haydn's proficiency as a composer of idiomatic vocal music had long been evident in his church music and operas. However, he was a late bloomer with regards to oratorio. *Il ritorno di Tobia* (1775, revised 1784) was an efficient but unremarkable work in the Metastasian style, and, although the composer's imagination was allegedly captured by hearing Handel's oratorios in London, his first stab at an oratorio after returning to Vienna was not particularly convincing. Instead of writing a completely new work, he adapted the scoring of his orchestral sonatas *The Seven Last Words* by adding clarinets and trombones, and superimposed sung texts for vocal soloists and choir. The result soon became popular in Vienna owing to regular performances by the Tonkünstler-Societät, and gradually supplanted the original orchestral version across Europe. It has been argued by scholars that the syllabic choral writing and lack of interesting contrapuntal detail make this version less effective than the remarkably contemplative mood of the original.

Haydn eventually received the chance to test his mettle as an oratorio composer of the first rank with *The Creation* (first performed in 1798). In Parts One and Two, the Archangels Gabriel (soprano), Uriel (tenor) and Raphael (bass) take turns to sing arias to narrate each of the six days of Creation as described in the Book of Genesis, with a few ideas thrown in from Milton's *Paradise Lost*: the dividing of light and darkness; the consternation of Lucifer and his followers; the formation of different elements of the weather; the divison of the world into oceans and land; the birth of the sun, moon and stars; the creation of plant, animal and human life. Haydn's sublime musical score illustrates each day with magnificent word-painting in accompanied recitatives and arias, and splendid concluding choral hymns of thanksgiving. In Part Three, Adam and Eve sing of their blissful state of innocence and love in the Garden of Eden. During the work we encounter music that ranks among the most radical, shocking, vividly descriptive, rapturous and (in the choruses) resplendent that Haydn ever wrote.

The Seasons (first performed 1801) was a deliberate attempt to repeat the same formula (a British poem adapted into German by Swieten; three soloists, choir and large orchestra; music that was essentially descriptive and pictorial), but it was probably less successful from an artistic point of view. Although its vitalising portrait of rural life against the background of the changing seasons has plenty of musical merit, it has often been argued, with good reason, that the oratorio is hampered by Swieten's clumsy adaptation of James Thomson's epic poem.

Personalities

Artaria Family: Viennese art dealers and map makers who from 1778 expanded into printing and selling music. The company became Haydn's main publisher from 1779 until the mid-1790s, after which the composer dealt primarily with Breitkopf & Härtel.

Bach, Carl Philipp Emanuel (1714–1788): Son of Johann Sebastian Bach. A prolific composer employed as a keyboard player at the court of Frederick the Great of Prussia (from 1738 to 1768), and then as Georg Philipp Telemann's successor as the city music director in Hamburg. C.P.E. Bach and Haydn never met, but the older man's music played a key part in shaping Haydn's musical personality in the 1760s.

Beethoven, Ludwig van (1770–1827): The difficult and volatile young composer studied composition under Haydn's supervision in the early 1790s. The relationship between the two greatest composers working in Vienna during the later 1790s and early 1800s was sometimes strained, though they seem to have remained admirers of each other's music.

Breitkopf & Härtel: Leipzig company that became Haydn's most important music publisher in the last decade of his life. Also founded the influential music journal *Allgemeine musikalische Zeitung* in 1796.

Burney, Charles (1726–1814): English music historian, composer, and teacher. Famed for his *General History of Music*, Burney became a close friend of Haydn during his trips to England, and later gave invaluable service to Haydn in gathering English subscriptions for the printed score of *The Creation*.

Dies, Albert Christoph (1755–1822): Professor of landscape painting at the Imperial Academy in Vienna. His biography of Haydn was based on conversations held with the aging composer between 15 April 1805 and 8 August 1808.

Dittersdorf, Carl Ditters von (1739–1799): Talented and versatile composer and violinist, and a good friend of Haydn. Once among the most popular composers in Europe, he died in poverty with his desk full of unwanted music.

Elssler, Johann Florian (1769–1843): The son of a music copyist at the Esterházy court, Johann started working for Haydn in about 1787 (five years after his father Joseph had died). He became Haydn's principal copyist and assistant, accompanied the composer during his second trip to England, and helped to compile his catalogue of compositions in 1805. Elssler and his wife lived with Haydn at Gumpendorf during the composer's last years, and received the largest single bequest from his will.

Esterházy family: From 1761 until the end of his life Haydn was employed by the wealthy and politically powerful Hungarian family, whose principal seat was at Eisenstadt. Haydn served under four reigning princes: Paul Anton Esterházy (1711–1762) engaged him as vice-Kapellmeister in 1761, but died soon afterwards. His brother Prince Nicolaus I (1714–1790) built an elaborate palace at Eszterháza and was a generous benefactor to Haydn. He was succeeded by his son Prince Anton (1738–1794), who dismissed almost the entire grand musical establishment (apart from Haydn, Tomasini, and a handful of others) and abandoned Eszterháza; his relationship with Haydn was cordial, appreciative and tolerant (Haydn spent most of Anton's short reign absent from his post while working in England). Haydn's last Esterházy employer, Prince Nicolaus II (1765–1833), led a dissolute lifestyle, and initially was on poor terms with his famous Kapellmeister. His wife, Princess Marie Hermenegild, was a loyal and kind friend to Haydn, and this influenced Nicolaus II's softening towards the aging composer.

Forster, William (1739–1808): London music publisher and string instrument maker, played a crucial role in making Haydn's music famous in England during the 1780s.

Genzinger, Maria Anna von (1750–1793): Wife of Prince Nicolaus Esterházy I's physician, and a talented amateur musician and close friend of Haydn for the last four years of her life. Their relationship was probably platonic, but certainly very affectionate.

Griesinger, Georg August (1769–1845): German diplomat and journalist who became a good friend of Haydn from 1799 until the composer's death. He was responsible for negotiating the composer's publications with Breitkopf & Härtel, who published his biography of Haydn in 1810.

Hasse, Johann Adolf (1699–1783): German-born composer who was the most influential opera composer across Europe for most of the middle decades of the eighteenth century. His music was especially popular in Vienna during the 1760s. Haydn sent a copy of his *Stabat mater* to Hasse, who predicted that he would be 'one of the greatest composers of the age'.

Haydn, Johann Evangelist (1743–1805): Joseph Haydn's youngest brother spent most of his life working as a church choir tenor for the Esterházys in Eisenstadt.

Haydn, (Johann) Michael (1737–1806): Haydn's younger brother shared a similar education at the choir school of St Stephen's Cathedral in Vienna under Reutter, and subsequently had a first-class education from the Jesuits. A fine composer in his own right, Michael was particularly respected for his outstanding church music. He spent most of his working life under-appreciated and underpaid in Salzburg, but for some reason rejected the Esterházys' invitation to become vice-Kapellmeister at Eisenstadt in the early 1800s.

Hummel, Johann Nepomuk (1778–1837): Prodigious composer and pianist who studied with Mozart and worked as concertmaster at Eisenstadt during Haydn's last years. He composed several fine masses for the Esterházys.

Keller, Maria Anna Aloysia Apollonia (1729–1800): Haydn's wife from 1760 until her death. The composer had first fallen in love with her younger sister Therese (whose parents insisted that she fulfil their vow for her to enter a nunnery). Maria Anna was unable to bear children, and the forty-year marriage was an unhappy one filled with infidelities from both partners.

Metastasio, Pietro (1698–1782): Imperial court poet in Vienna, and celebrated librettist whose works were set by every major opera composer of the eighteenth century, from Handel to Mozart. He was supportive towards his close neighbour Haydn at the beginning of the musician's freelance career in the 1750s.

Mozart, Wolfgang Amadeus (1756–1791): Although Mozart and Haydn undoubtedly knew about each other through their music (and Mozart's friendship with Haydn's brother Michael at Salzburg), there is no evidence that they became close friends until 1784. Haydn was often generous in his praise and recommendation of Mozart to other musicians and patrons, and was distraught at the news of the younger man's death in December 1791.

Pleyel, Ignaz (1757–1831): After Beethoven, Haydn's most successful pupil. An excellent violinist and popular composer, Pleyel was embarrassed to find that he had been set up in competition against his old teacher in London during the 1792 concert season. The two men remained loyal friends. Pleyel settled in Paris and increasingly devoted his energies to music publishing.

Polzelli, Luigia (1750–1831): A soprano of little distinction in the Eszterháza opera company from 1779 until its disbandment in 1790, Polzelli was Haydn's mistress. Haydn later taught both her sons, Pietro and Antonio, and assisted them in their careers. Luigia claimed that Antonio was Haydn's son; the composer never commented on the matter, but frequently sent her money and remained in touch with her for the rest of his life, even after their relationship had evidently fizzled out.

Porpora, Nicola (1686–1768): Renowned opera composer and singing teacher, who had taught the famous castrato Farinelli and worked in competition against Handel's opera company in London during the mid-1730s. A friend of Metastasio, who introduced him to Haydn. Haydn served as Porpora's valet and keyboard accompanist, and reputedly learned much from the old master while he was in Vienna.

Reutter, Georg (1708–1772): Kapellmeister of St Stephen's Cathedral in Vienna, composer of church music, and Haydn's teacher. Having studied under Antonio Caldara and worked with Johann Joseph Fux, Reutter was a disciplined musician who, despite giving the young choirboy Haydn little formal training, exposed him to decisive musical influences and experiences.

Salomon, Johann Peter (1745–1815): German-born violinist who knew C.P.E. Bach in Berlin and the child Beethoven in Bonn; Salomon was an active musician in London and seized the initiative to bring Haydn to England after Prince Nicolaus Esterházy I's death in 1790. Salomon experienced mixed fortunes as a concert series promoter, but the legacy from his friendship with Haydn is enormous: all twelve 'London' symphonies and several string quartets were written for Salomon, who also provided Haydn with the manuscript libretto for *The Creation*.

Schroeter, Rebecca (1751–1826): Widow of the composer Johann Samuel Schroeter, she settled in London in 1786. She became a close friend of Haydn soon after he arrived in England, and it is highly likely that they became lovers. Haydn later confided to Dies that he would have married her had he been free to do so, but after his first trip to London no correspondence between them survives (during his second visit they lived close to each other, making correspondence unnecessary).

Swieten, (Baron) Gottfried van (1733–1803): Born at Leiden in the Netherlands, Swieten was the son of the distinguished doctor Gerhard van Swieten. The family moved to Vienna in 1745 when his father was appointed personal physician to Empress Maria Theresa. As a young man in Vienna, Brussels and Paris, Swieten was an active amateur musician (two of his comic operas and at least seven of his symphonies survive), and he developed into a notably influential figure in Viennese musical circles. In 1773 he commissioned six symphonies for strings from C.P.E. Bach. Swieten's passion for Handel and J.S. Bach was a major influence on Mozart's musical style in the composer's last years, and the Baron provided the librettos for Haydn's two great oratorios *The Creation* and *The Seasons*. Swieten was the dedicatee of Beethoven's Symphony No. 1 and Forkel's pioneering biography of Bach.

Tomasini, Luigi (1741–1808): Probably employed at the Esterházy court from about 1752–3 as Prince Paul Anton's page, Tomasini was sponsored by the Prince to study violin playing in Venice (1759) and with Leopold Mozart in Salzburg (1760). In 1761, at about the same time as Haydn was engaged by the Prince, Tomasini was officially added to the payroll as a violinist, and soon became the leader and concertmaster of the Capelle.

Werner, Gregor Joseph (1693–1766): Haydn's predecessor as the Esterházys' Kapellmeister was appointed in 1728. He diligently developed the quality and performance standards of church music at Eisenstadt, where he composed over twenty oratorios. Infirm and confined to his rooms during the early 1760s, Werner had little musical interaction with his vice-Kapellmeister Haydn, to whom he grew resentful.

Selected Bibliography

Clark, C., ed., *The Cambridge Companion to Haydn*, Cambridge, 2005

Dies, A.C., *Biographische Nachrichten von Joseph Haydn*, Vienna, 1810; Eng. trans. in Gotwals

Geiringer, K., *Haydn: a Creative Life in Music*, New York, 1946; third (revised) edition, 1982

Gotwals, V., ed., *Joseph Haydn: Eighteenth-Century Gentleman and Genius*, Madison, 1963

Griesinger, G.A., *Biographische Notizen über Joseph Haydn*, Leipzig, 1810, rev. 1819; Eng. trans. in Gotwals

Hoboken, A. van, *Joseph Haydn: thematisch-bibliographisches Werkverzeichnis*,
  i: *Instrumentalwerke*;
  ii: *Vokalwerke*;
  iii: *Register: Addenda und Corrigenda*, Mainz, 1957–78

Hughes, R., *Haydn*, London, 1950; sixth edition, 1989

Jones, D.W., ed., *Oxford Composer Companions: Haydn*, Oxford, 2002

Landon, H.C.R., *Haydn: Chronicle and Works*,
  i: *Haydn: the Early Years 1732–1765* (London, 1980);
  ii: *Haydn at Eszterháza 1766–1790* (1978);
  iii: *Haydn in England 1791–1795* (1976);
  iv: *Haydn: the Years of 'The Creation' 1796–1800* (1977);
  v: *Haydn: the Late Years 1801–1809* (1977)
  - *Haydn: a Documentary Study*, London, 1981
  - (ed.) *The Collected Correspondence and London Notebooks of Joseph Haydn*, London, 1959

Landon, H.C.R., & Jones, D.W., *Haydn: his Life and Music*, London, 1988

Sutcliffe, W.D., *Haydn: String Quartets, Op. 50*, Cambridge, 1992

Temperley, N., *Haydn: 'The Creation'*, Cambridge, 1991

Webster, J., & Feder, G., *The New Grove Haydn*, London, 2002

Glossary

Adagio Slow.

Allegro Fast, but not excessively so.

Andante Gracefully, at a moderate walking pace.

Aria Solo song, usually part of a cantata, opera or oratorio, although Haydn wrote some free-standing 'concert arias' and self-contained operatic scenes (e.g. *Berenice, che fai?*).

Bass The lowest-sounding musical participant in either a vocal or instrumental ensemble; also the lowest register of solo voice.

Cadenza A relatively brief, occasionally showy solo of improvisatory character that usually heralds the orchestral close to a concerto movement or an opera aria. Haydn disliked singers producing excessive ornamentation and cadenzas in his late vocal works.

Cantata A work in several movements for voice (or voices), usually accompanied by orchestra. Shorter than an oratorio, but not necessarily performed by smaller forces. The term should not be exclusively associated with music composed for religious services; Haydn wrote several 'secular' cantatas for Prince Nicolaus Esterházy I. Haydn's *Arianna a Naxos* is a rare example of a cantata accompanied only by piano.

Capelle 'Chapel', but also a term describing the musical establishment at the Esterházy court.

Concerto A work for solo instrument and orchestra, generally in three movements (fast–slow–fast).

Continuo In eighteenth-century music it was common for a harpsichord (later a fortepiano) to supply semi-improvised accompaniments in fully orchestrated or vocal music. The player would read the written-out bass part, and, using his experience of harmony, would fill out the middle of the musical texture. Especially vital in recitatives. In Haydn's operas and oratorios, simple recitatives were accompanied by a 'continuo' section including keyboard and solo cello.

Counterpoint The interweaving of separate 'horizontal' melodic lines, as opposed to the accompaniment of a top-line ('horizontal') melody by a series of ('vertical') chords.

Fantasia A free form, often improvisatory, rather than adhering to a pre-ordained structure.

Feld-harmonie The Esterházy band of woodwind and brass instruments.

Finale A generic term for 'last movement'.

Forte / Fortissimo Loud; very loud.

Fortepiano 'Loud-soft', the name given to the early pianos known to Haydn. These instruments were smaller and quieter than modern grand pianos.

Fugue An imitative work in several overlapping parts (vocal or instrumental).

Harmony The simultaneous sounding of notes to make a chord, or the way in which contrapuntal lines (see 'Counterpoint') interweave to produce an overall sound.

Harpsichord A keyboard instrument in which the strings are plucked rather than struck. The instrument gradually fell from favour during the latter half of the eighteenth century, and was replaced by the fortepiano.

Kapellmeister 'Chapel master', the respectful term given to the head of musical establishments in Austria and Germany, derived from the Italian title *maestro di cappella*. A Kapellmeister was expected to be entirely responsible for managing all aspects of musical life in aristocratic and ecclesiastical institutions.

Mass The Roman Catholic liturgical text for Sunday Eucharist services. The Latin words were often set to music for special feast days and celebratory occasions. During the eighteenth century a full-scale 'solemn' mass (*Missa solemnis*) was normally divided into five sections: Kyrie, Gloria, Credo, Sanctus-Benedictus and Agnus Dei; the shorter form of the mass (*Missa brevis*) sometimes only included the first two sections.

Minuet Originally a French folk dance, an ancestor of the waltz, considered to be an elegant and cultivated musical form.

Obbligato A term describing the 'obligatory' role of a solo instrument or group of solo instruments in a context where such a role is not normally expected. The solo organ in Haydn's 'Little Organ Mass' is one such 'obbligato' part.

Opera buffa An Italian genre of 'comic' opera that became dominant in the late eighteenth century; Mozart and other composers preferred the more ambiguous and literary label 'dramma giocoso'. Most of Haydn's operas fit into this category.

Opera seria 'Serious' opera, often more elevated, tragic or heroic than 'opera buffa'. Haydn wrote very few serious operas. This was not an indication of his personal taste, but a reflection of the entertainment preferred by the Esterházy family.

Oratorio An extended choral–orchestral setting of religious texts in a dramatic and semi-operatic fashion. Although it was originally an Italian genre, Handel invented a unique style of English oratorio that influenced Haydn to write his late works *The Creation* and *The Seasons*.

Piano / Pianissimo Soft, very soft.

Pizzicato Plucked strings.

Recitative A short section in which a solo voice (or several, taking turns) carry forward the plot or narrative in cantatas, operas and oratorios. Recitatives serve as introductions to the next aria, duet, ensemble or chorus. The rhythm is dictated by the words. There are two types. 1: Simple ('semplice', or 'secco') recitative is accompanied only by keyboard and cello (see 'Continuo'); 2: Accompanied ('accompagnato') recitative, in which the composer provides an elaborate orchestrated accompaniment for special dramatic or illustrative effect (e.g. most of the recitatives in *The Creation*).

Sonata A term used to describe a short composition (usually for a solo instrument, but also sometimes for a small group) that normally consists of three movements presenting a contrast in character. The first movement would normally be in 'sonata form' (see below), the central movement would be slower, and followed by a concluding rondo or similarly appropriate finale. Some sonatas would feature an extra penultimate movement, such as a 'minuet'.

Sonata form The dominant formal structure of instrumental music throughout the second half of the eighteenth century. A 'sonata-form' movement is divided into three sections: 1: exposition (introducing the main theme or themes); 2: development (during which the themes are varied and dissected); 3: recapitulation (the return of the exposition in a refined and more adventurous form leading to a conclusion in the home key).

Soprano The highest solo or choral voice. In eighteenth-century operas, high vocal parts were often sung by castratos, although Haydn's comic operas at Eszterháza seldom required anything other than 'natural' high female voices.

String Quartet A sonata for two violins, viola and cello, normally in four movements; also the name of the instrumental group playing the music.

Symphony A sonata for orchestra, normally in four movements.

Tempo The pace of music.

Tenor The second lowest male voice in a choral texture, and often the kind of solo voice used for lovers and heroes in Haydn's operas. In the eighteenth century 'tenor' was also used to describe the viola.

Variations   A movement in which a short theme is subjected to a series of decorated repetitions and, occasionally, more radical transformations. A common form for solo keyboard music in the late-eighteenth century.

Annotations of CD Tracks

CD 1

☐ Symphony No. 6 in D major ('Le Matin'). **Movement 1: Adagio – Allegro**

Unlike the nicknames of many popular Haydn symphonies, those of No. 6 ('Le Matin'), No. 7 ('Le Midi') and No. 8 ('Le Soir') are authentic. The idea for programmatic symphonies depicting different times of the day was suggested to Haydn by Prince Paul Anton Esterházy (whose music library contained many Italian Baroque works such as Vivaldi's *Four Seasons*). Haydn's three symphonies reflect old-fashioned Italian Baroque styles, with two solo violins and one cello grouped together to provide a contrast with the full forces available, much as composers fifty years earlier had used such contrasts in concerti grossi. 'Le Matin' commences with a sleepy *Adagio*, a short section only eight bars long that is perhaps an evocation of sunrise, with a single line unfurling into a glorious *tutti* (similar to the moment depicting the birth of the stars in *The Creation*, which was composed the best part of four decades later (see CD 2, track 11)). It is followed by a spirited *Allegro*, in which the theme is initiated by flute, emulated by oboe, and taken over by the entire band. Bassoons and horns also add colour to the texture.

☐ Symphony No. 7 in C major ('Le Midi'). **Movement 4: Finale: Allegro**

Haydn portrays a lively afternoon, led by two solo violins. Each of these three symphonies features plentiful opportunities to display the virtuoso members of the Esterházy band, in particular its concertmaster Luigi Tomasini (Haydn probably played the secondary solo violin part). In the finale of No. 7, a solo flute is given its turn to sparkle with some brilliant virtuoso passages. Although this is one of Haydn's earliest surviving major works, it is notable that his witty playfulness and extrovert inventiveness are already fully fledged.

181

3 Symphony No. 8 in G major ('Le Soir'). **Movement 4: La tempesta: Presto**

'Le Soir' does not portray a quiet evening, but one of public splendour and court gaiety. However, Haydn introduces some jovial theatricality for the finale, *La tempesta*. This *Presto* movement commences with an agitated solo violin, which within a few seconds is joined by the rest of the violins; Haydn then adds two punctuating horns, and then a moment later two oboes. The full band is rapidly brought into play, with lightning vividly evoked by a solo flute, before Haydn takes us to a suitably thrilling conclusion.

4 – 5 Keyboard Sonata in G major (Hob.XVI:6)
Movement 3: Adagio
Movement 4: Finale: Allegro molto

Haydn's keyboard music written during the late 1750s and early 1760s was created for and played on harpsichords. Some small-scale sonatas and sets of variations were essentially technical exercises that remain useful to piano students today, but the scholar Michelle Fillion has written that Haydn's grander solo keyboard sonatas of this period are 'brilliantly conceived for the harpsichord, and exude a rugged vitality and breadth of expression'. During the composer's long career the old plucked-string instrument was gradually replaced by the recently invented fortepiano, which used hammers to strike the strings and allowed greater dynamic flexibility. This keyboard sonata was probably written in about 1760, and its autograph manuscript is the earliest-known authentic source of Haydn's keyboard compositions. The beautiful *Adagio* has a melancholic atmosphere, produced by a Bachian melody flowing over gently repeated chords. The delicacy and tenderness of the *Adagio* is deliberately contrasted with the brilliant finale, which is packed with sparkling fast passages.

6 Cello Concerto No. 1 in C major (Hob.VIIb:1). **Movement 1: Moderato**

The Esterházy 'Capelle' included several outstanding musicians capable of playing demanding solo parts in concertos. Haydn's dazzling yet lyrical writing for solo cello was tailor-made for the extraordinary cellist Joseph Weigl. The courtly C major

Moderato of the first movement features springy 'Lombard' rhythms and impressive tricks designed to show Weigl's technical ability, but the music also allowed the soloist to demonstrate his judgement and taste; Haydn's composition is not merely a showy display piece for Weigl, but a poetic statement possessing melodic charm and elegant beauty. The long unaccompanied solo cadenza towards the end of the movement is a modern invention played by Ludovít Kanta, but there can be little doubt that Haydn expected Weigl to provide an unaccompanied flourish at this point. This concerto is one of the young Haydn's finest masterpieces, but it was never published in his own lifetime and was rediscovered at Prague in 1962.

7̄ Symphony No. 49 in F minor ('La passione'). **Movement 4: Finale: Presto**

Composed in 1768 for the Esterházy Capelle (probably whilst it was still based in Eisenstadt), this symphony is set by Haydn in the unusual key of F minor, and adopts the old Baroque form known as 'sonata da chiesa' ('church sonata'): four movements, with the pattern slow – quick – slow (minuet) – quick. The relentlessly driven finale, with throbbing repeated quavers played by the cellos and double basses, is one of Haydn's finest attempts to convey increasing tension and tempestuous emotion of all his *Sturm und Drang* symphonies composed during the late 1760s and early 1770s. The nickname 'La passione' was probably invented by a Leipzig law student who inscribed it on his manuscript copy of the score.

8̄ Baryton Trio in D major (Hob.XI:11). **Movement 3: Finale: Presto**

Although this performance features two violins and a cello, Haydn intended the lower part to be played by the baryton. This was an unusual seven-stringed instrument that had a fretted fingerboard and gut strings like a viola da gamba (a member of the viol family considered archaic by the 1760s), but with wire strings behind the fingerboard that vibrated with the bowed gut strings or that could be plucked by the left hand. This short *Presto*, full of witty gestures and lively interplay between the three instruments, was composed before 1772. One imagines that Tomasini and Haydn played the violin parts, and it is likely that the baryton part was played either by Prince Nicolaus Esterházy I (a talented amateur musician and an avid fan of the

183

baryton) or by the professional baryton player Andreas Lidl who was employed at Eszterháza.

9 Symphony No. 45 in F sharp minor ('Farewell'). **Movement 4: Presto – Adagio**

Haydn and his musicians did not universally approve of having to spend most of the year at Prince Nicolaus's remote new castle at Eszterháza. In 1772, after an extended 'summer' stay that turned into ten months, the musicians were desperate to return to Eisenstadt. Haydn communicated this diplomatically to the Prince in the composition of this symphony. It uses the bizarre key of F sharp minor and contains some unusually angry music in the first movement, after which it resolves in a particularly touching and serious manner. At first the finale is a tempestuous *Presto*, but, after a short pause, the music transforms into an *Adagio* (symphonies almost never ended with slow movements, so this will have grabbed the Prince's attention). After a solo passage, the first oboe and second horn players leave the room (after having blown out their candles). Then the bassoonist departs after a short solo. The formula is repeated by the second oboe and first horn, and even the double bass is given a short solo before it also disappears from view. By the end only two violins remain (Haydn and Tomasini), who end with some very soft staccato notes, blow out their candles, and exit.

10 L'infedeltà delusa. **Act II, Finale: 'Nel mille settecento'**

Haydn's *opera buffa* is set to a libretto by Marco Coltellini, who presents a tale of how deceit is outwitted (or, more literally, how an 'unfaithful' lover is 'deluded'). Two pairs of lovers (Vespina and Nencio, Sandrina and Nanni) are peasants whose lives are thrown into disorder by Sandrina's father Filippo, who wants his daughter to marry Nencio (who agrees). Angry at the fickle Nencio and determined not to be outwitted, the cunning Vespina successfully discredits him by spreading slanderous reports that he seduced and abandoned a young woman. In the opera's finale, Vespina is disguised as a notary who has arrived to draw up the marriage contract between Sandrina and the Marchese di Ripafratta (who, naturally, does not really exist: the aristocrat whom Filippo hopes will bring financial prosperity is in fact one of Vespina's three previous disguises). Nencio and Nanni both sign as witnesses (although only Nanni is in on the joke); Vespina discards her disguise, reveals her deception by quoting phrases from each of her previous disguises (which also include an old crone and a drunken German maidservant), and triumphantly informs the meddling Filippo and unfaithful Nencio that their plotting has failed. Reconciled and reunited, the two pairs of lovers can now celebrate a double wedding. Haydn's fast-moving music captures Vespina's scheming control over events, and brings the drama to a superbly colourful conclusion.

11 Il ritorno di Tobia ('The Return of Tobias'). **Part 2, Chorus: 'Svanisce in un momento'**

The libretto for *Il ritorno di Tobia* ('The Return of Tobias') was written by Giovanni Gastone Boccherini (brother of the famous composer, and whose family were well-known in Viennese musical circles). The story is taken from the apocryphal Book of Tobit, in which the titular character is a blind old man whose eyesight is miraculously restored. Newspaper reports compared three grand choruses to music by Handel; although it is unlikely that Haydn knew much about Handel's music in the early 1770s, it is certain the Austrian modernist had been influenced by composers (Caldara, Porpora and Hasse) whose music was familiar to the great English oratorio composer. In the chorus 'Svanisce in un momento', a tempestuous orchestral introduction featuring braying horns is followed by highly charged and dramatically shaded choral passages. One of the most exciting parts of Haydn's oratorio, it was an addition composed for the Tonkünstler-Societät's revival in 1784.

12 Symphony No. 70 in D major. **Movement 4: Allegro con brio**

Falling in between the so-called *Sturm und Drang* period and Haydn's grander symphonies for Paris and London, the symphonies composed during the later 1770s are often unfairly neglected. One masterpiece from these years is Symphony No. 70 in D, a celebratory work written for the ceremony on 18 December 1779 in which the foundation stone was laid for the rebuilding of the Eszterháza opera house. Flamboyantly scored for flute, oboes, bassoon, horns, trumpets, timpani and strings, the finale is, surprisingly, a minor-key fugue of intense seriousness and learnedness.

185

It features striking use of a repeated five-note figure. It was remarkable that Haydn chose this as the climax to a major-keyed symphony created for a commemorative occasion. H.C. Robbins Landon suggested that the agitated D minor opening was intended as a programmatic description of the raging flames that had devastated the theatre, and that the eventual D major conclusion signifies 'the happy event for which the work was composed'.

13 Missa brevis Sancti Joannis de Deo ('Little Organ Mass'). **Benedictus**

One of Haydn's most intimate small-scale mass settings, this was probably composed in winter 1777 for the tiny Eisenstadt chapel of the Barmherzige Brüder. Scored for only two violins, four voices (soprano, alto, tenor and bass), and continuo, it is highly likely that Haydn expected it to be performed by only eight or nine performers (depending on whether the cello part was also played by double bass). The exquisite setting of the Benedictus is for solo soprano and organ obbligato (which Haydn probably played himself), with occasional rhetorical contributions from the violins and lower strings. Owing to its limited musical resources, the 'Little Organ Mass' was within the capacity of most church musical establishments, and thus became one of Haydn's most popular compositions within his own lifetime.

14 Symphony No. 83 in G minor ('The Hen'). **Movement 4: Vivace**

This 'Paris' symphony is one of Haydn's most convivial and deliciously ironic orchestral compositions, notwithstanding its opening key of G minor (often associated with far more solemn emotional expressions, especially in Haydn's church music). It became known as 'The Hen' during the nineteenth century because of the clucking four-note motif used extensively in the opening movement. The last movement is a merry dance in 12/8, which skips along nonchalantly whilst presenting a strongly flavoured mischievous personality. H.C. Robbins Landon suggested that this humorous conclusion to a minor-key symphony was a deliberate move away from the earnest *Sturm und Drang* writing that Haydn had cultivated over a decade earlier. It is a fine illustration of Haydn's ability to joke with the listener's expectations (a solo flute passage when one expects full orchestra; a lurch into skittish rhythms, or unpredictable modulations) whilst investing the music with amazingly fertile invention and technical substance.

15 String Quartet in D major, Op. 50 No. 6 ('The Frog') (Hob.HIII:49)
Movement 3: Menuetto: Allegretto

As well as a symphonic innovator, Haydn is often regarded as the 'Father of the String Quartet'. W.D. Sutcliffe has pointed out that the string quartet 'was subject to few of the constraints that external circumstances could impose upon the composer in other genres: the varying constitution of the eighteenth-century orchestra, the need to keep keyboard sonatas and trios within the stylistic and technical limits of a largely amateur market, or the many and varied limitations set on the composition of sacred music'. Intended as private music for true musical connoisseurs, Haydn's Op. 50 – dedicated to King Friedrich Wilhelm II of Prussia – was serious art music. The adventurous and highly chromatic sixth quartet is widely considered the richest and most ambitious of the set. The third of its four movements is one of Haydn's most attractive minuets, which is a dance-like triple-time movement. After the main theme, with its 'scotch-snap' style rhythms from the leading violin, Haydn creates subtle modulations and varies his treatment of the theme in ways that frequently eschew predictability. Only towards the end of the minuet does the theme return for one brief restatement.

CD 2

① Piano Sonata in E flat major (Hob.XVI:49). **Movement 2: Adagio e cantabile**

The long slow movement of this piano sonata, marked *Cantabile* ('in a singing style'), is exceptionally beautiful. The synthesis of delicacy and melancholic depth shows Haydn exploring the kind of emotional territory evident in Mozart's most yearning music. Although dedicated to Prince Nicolaus Esterházy I's housekeeper Anna de Jerlischek, the sonata was actually written for Haydn's friend Maria Anna von Genzinger, who must have been an accomplished pianist of both skill and taste. However, a section in which left and right hands cross over apparently caused Frau Genzinger difficulty. It is possible that Haydn rewrote the movement for her, or coached her on its performance during one of his trips to Vienna.

② Orfeo ed Euridice (L'anima del filosofo). **Act III, Scene 3: 'Al tuo seno fortunato'**

Based on the Greek myth of the musician Orpheus seeking to reclaim his dead wife Eurydice, Haydn's last and most tragic opera was his first major composition for London in 1791. However, the opera was never performed in Haydn's own lifetime (it was first staged in Florence in 1951). Act III commences with Orpheus's lament at Eurydice's grave, after which he visits a spirit ('Genio', or 'Sibyl') in a cave near the entrance to Hades. The Genio promises to lead him to the underworld, and encourages him to reclaim the spirit of his wife. 'Al tuo seno fortunato' is the most brilliant heroic aria in the opera, with bold orchestration (including the splendid combination of trumpets, horns and drums) and astonishing long passages of difficult coloratura for the singer (probably the soprano castrato Dorelli), who promises Orpheus 'To your fortunate breast you shall clasp the one you love, if you will arm your heart with constancy and valour'.

3 Symphony No. 92 in G major ('Oxford'). **Movement 2: Adagio**

Performed in Oxford on 7 July 1791, the day before Haydn accepted a Doctorate from the city's famous university, this symphony gained its nickname during the nineteenth century. It was composed in 1789 (probably at Eszterháza) as part of a group of three symphonies (Nos 90–92) that fulfilled commissions from the Prince of Oettingen in Germany and the Parisian concert promoter Comte d'Ogny (who must have wanted to capitalise on the recent success of Haydn's six 'Paris' symphonies). Without doubt one of Haydn's greatest artistic achievements, the expansive slow movement in D major features poignant wind-band solo passages, and the use of noisier trumpets and drums in the minor-keyed middle section creates a distinctive contrast. The rhapsodic return of the first section is varied and decorated beyond its original form, with even more emphasis placed on the emotionally telling contributions of the woodwind. It is little wonder that after its first London performance the local press reported with astonishment that Haydn 'moves and governs the passions at his will'.

4 Symphony No. 94 in G major ('The Surprise'). **Movement 2: Andante**

This famous symphony was composed for London and first performed on 23 March 1792 at the Hanover Square Rooms. There are differing anecdotes about why Haydn wanted to 'surprise' his audience with an unexpected loud chord that disturbs the child-like theme of the slow movement. One eyewitness claimed that Haydn had pointed to the score and said 'There the ladies will jump', whereas his biographer Dies claimed that some members of Haydn's audience fell asleep during slow movements and so the composer wanted to shock them from their slumber. The truth might be less theatrical: Haydn told Griesinger that he had merely wanted to surprise the audience by trying something new. It is certain that Haydn's 'surprise' loud chord was a late insertion after he had completed the score. But the music, as is typical of Haydn's 'London' symphonies generally, is packed with all kinds of smaller surprises: the theme is masterfully treated with intelligently deployed orchestral resources, differently coloured accompaniments, several contrasting styles, and at one point a dramatic change from C major to C minor. Although it ranks among

Haydn's most familiar compositions (he parodied it himself in Simon's ploughman's song in *The Seasons*), there are few such obvious examples of his remarkably fertile musical imagination.

5 Symphony No. 104 in D major ('London'). **Movement 4: Finale: Spiritoso**

Haydn's twelfth symphony composed especially for Salomon's London concerts turned out to be his last ever symphony; thereafter he strenuously resisted all inducements to write any more. Since his early orchestral works for the Esterházy Capelle, Haydn's pioneering musical vocabulary had evolved a long way, and in this spirited finale it is possible to discern the sixty-three-year-old composer passing on the torch to Beethoven. For example, the rustic drones, flamboyant use of a large orchestral canvas, and patiently sustained dramatic rhetorical character are comparable to Beethoven's Symphony No. 6 ('Pastoral'). It has been alleged that the main theme of the finale was inspired by London street cries selling fish or cakes, but it might also have been based on a Croatian folksong familiar to Haydn from his years at Eszterháza. It is typical of Haydn's genius that he could take such a humble idea and turn it into one of his most spectacular and dazzling climaxes.

6 Trumpet Concerto in E flat major (Hob.VIIe:1). **Movement 3: Allegro**

This was composed in 1796 after Haydn's return from London to Vienna. It was written for Anton Weidinger, who had recently invented a new kind of keyed trumpet that could, unlike conventional natural trumpets, play chromatic melodies. Haydn's writing reveals that Weidinger must have been a gifted player capable of impressive flexibility and eloquent execution of difficult passages, and Haydn was fascinated by the possibilities offered by the new type of trumpet (every note which it was capable of playing is featured somewhere in the concerto). This proved to be Haydn's last purely orchestral composition, and is an intriguing fusion of Viennese Classical elegance and the large-scale orchestral scoring Haydn had encountered in London. The finale contains sophisticated melodic passages for trumpet which had scarcely been heard since the heyday of high trumpet playing in the Baroque era of Bach and Handel (although neither of these composers had been able to write chromatically for the trumpets of their day). However, Haydn also retained the familiar trumpet element of repeated-note fanfares.

7 String Quartet, Op. 76 No. 3 ('Emperor') (Hob.HIII:77)
Movement 2: Poco adagio, cantabile

Nicknamed 'Emperor' by the British during the nineteenth century, this elegant *cantabile* ('singing-style') sequence of variations is based on Haydn's *Volkslied*, which had been commissioned as the Austrian national anthem as the Napoleonic wars loomed over the Habsburg Empire. Op. 76 was one of Haydn's last major collections of instrumental music, and in his years of failing health he repeatedly played this movement on the piano. Curiously, the use of this slow and sweetly elegant theme as the Austrian national anthem was banned after the First World War, by which time it had been adopted by the Germans, who today usually play it in a bombastic orchestration far removed from Haydn's original.

8 Missa in angustiis ('Nelson Mass') (Hob.HXXII:11). Kyrie

In his later years Haydn composed little for his employers the Esterházy family, but five of his late six mass settings were specifically composed for the nameday celebration services of Princess Marie Hermenegild (which normally took place in early September at the Bergkirche in Eisenstadt). The opening Kyrie eleison of the so-called 'Nelson Mass' is an unusually troubled and impassioned plea for the Lord to have mercy on the penitent worshippers. Using the dark D minor tonality (established with a rapid yet bleak descending arpeggio from the strings), tense choral exclamations and fervent (perhaps even frantic) interjections from a solo soprano are interwoven with melodramatic string writing and three trumpets playing unison fanfares. The tense opening gambit of Haydn's most openly dramatic church music must have astonished (and presumably impressed) the Esterházys. The rest of the mass is equally spectacular, most notably a blazing militaristic trumpet fanfare in the Benedictus. Despite its nickname and troubled tone, the work has no known connection with either the Napoleonic wars or Lord Admiral Nelson.

9 – 10 Die Jahreszeiten ('The Seasons')

Autumn: Recitative: 'Hier ein dichter Kreis die Hasen'

Autumn: Chorus: 'Hört, hört das laute Getön'

In Haydn's last oratorio, each of the four seasons is depicted with associated nature imagery and human actions. In 'Autumn' different social classes of hunters are portrayed. In an accompanied recitative, Lucas (tenor) describes peasants trapping hares (the orchestra illustrates the scurrying animals), and the recitative resolves as the hares are captured and laid out in rows to be counted. Suddenly, the scene is interrupted by the sound of aristocratic hunting horns: lordly hunters are pursuing a stag. The chorus gleefully describes how the mountains, vales and forests resound with the sound of hounds, hunters and their horns. Four horns play authentic horn signals that hunters in Haydn's audience would have recognised, violas and bassoons emulate barking hounds, and the rushing strings portray the fleeing stag.

11 – 12 Die Schöpfung ('The Creation')

Part I, No. 12: 'In vollem Glanze steiget jetzt die Sonne' (Uriel)

Part I, No. 13: 'Die Himmel erzählen die Ehre Gottes' (Gabriel, Uriel, Raphael, Chorus)

Parts I and II of Haydn's oratorio feature musical illustrations of each of the six creative periods as described in the biblical Book of Genesis. During the fourth day God divides day from night and creates stars in the heavens. To evoke the glorious sunrise of the first morning, Haydn uses a similar device to that of his 'Le Matin' Symphony (see CD 1, track 1): a single note (played by unison clarinet and violins) unfurls step by step into mysterious suspended harmonies, gradually expanding until it resolves on a full chord and bursts into radiant sunshine with a full orchestral climax (including brass and timpani). This forms a remarkable introduction to an accompanied recitative for the angel Uriel (tenor), who announces that the sun has now risen in full splendour. In a very quiet second section, Uriel softly describes the contrasting moonlight and the numberless stars that make up the vaulted ceiling of the heavens (the stillness of night is portrayed by the lower strings of the orchestra). Uriel then introduces a chorus of 'the sons of God', who rejoice that the sun, moon, stars, and passage of day and night testify God's greatness ('The Heavens are telling the glory of God'). The chorus alternates full choral sections with solo trios for the angels Gabriel (soprano), Uriel (tenor) and Raphael (bass); after the second trio finishes dramatically, the chorus accelerates towards an excited fugue ('Und seiner Hände Werk') that forms a dynamic climax to Part I of the oratorio.

13   Die Schöpfung ('The Creation')
Part III, No. 30: 'Von deiner Güt', o Herr und Gott' (Eve and Adam, Chorus)

The third and final part of *The Creation* portrays Adam and Eve in a state of purity and innocence in the Garden of Eden (prior to their succumbing to temptation and being cast out; their 'fall' is alluded to by Uriel at the end of the oratorio). The dramatic pace of the action slows down, but the score of this section contains some of Haydn's most sublime and heartfelt music. In Adam and Eve's duet 'Von deiner Güt" ('By thee with bliss'), over a gently lilting accompaniment featuring a tender oboe solo, the newly created couple praises the vast and wonderful world that God has granted to them. A chorus of angels softly echoes Adam and Eve's sentiments, with syncopated refrains 'Forever blessed be thy power'. When this rapturous duet concludes, the movement is far from over: Haydn then proceeds to a more extrovert duet section, filled with joyous outbursts from the chorus and glorious flourishes from the full orchestra. As the praise becomes increasingly ecstatic, Haydn takes the opportunity to play games with the listener. Material is sustained and developed, and just when one imagines the final climax is near, Haydn does something else wonderfully unpredictable. When this movement is perceived as a single structure, it is clear that Haydn deliberately progresses from an intimate, leisurely duet to an overwhelming *tour de force* of irrepressible musical spirit.

Index

W

Y

Z

Also Available

Mozart

Beethoven

Chopin

Mahler

Also Available

Tchaikovsky

Wagner

Puccini

Dvořák